MW00905961

A COLLEGE WOMEN'S STUDY

DELIGHT YOURSELF IN THE LORD, AND HE WILL GIVE YOU THE DESIRES OF YOUR HEART
PSALM 37:4

TABLE OF CONTENTS

Rachel H : *Choosing Vulnerability*   No. 17

Rachel L : *Act of Surrender*   No. 29

Brianna : *Joyfully Obedient*   No. 43

Shelby : *Overcoming Jealousy*   No. 53

Reggie : *An Authentic Christian*   No. 65

Madi : *Overwhelming Grace*   No. 77

Morgan : *Trusting God's Sovereignty*   No. 89

Sydney : *Trusting His Story*   No. 101

Andrea : *Never Losing Faith*   No. 115

Erin : *Choosing to Rejoice*   No. 129

OUR MISSION

Inviting college women into Christ-centered community that fosters vulnerability and transforms stories.

WHO WE ARE

We are a college women's community that grows together, serves together, learns together, and does life together while chasing the heart of God.

WHAT WE DO

We provide college women with the tools and resources to launch, grow and sustain Christ-centered communities on college campuses. We create curriculum that tells the real stories of college women chasing the heart of God.

OUR STORY

We here at Delight are big believers in stories. Stories that move and inspire, take our breath away, stop us in our tracks, and change us forever. Delight was created as a platform for college women to not only share their stories but also as a place to allow God to write stories more beautiful than we could ever even fathom.

SO LET US TELL YOU THE STORY OF DELIGHT.

Two freshmen girls meet at Belmont University and become best friends. On the last day of freshmen year the two girls go to dinner with another girl. Girls talk the whole time about how AWESOME God is. The three girls go home for summer. One girl works as a waitress. One girl goes to Alaska for a mission experience. Other girl sells knives. Girls return in the fall. Girls go to church together. On the way home waitress girl asks the other two girls if they want to start a bible study. Other two girls say yes because they both felt the same nudging over the summer. Girls meet in the bell tower on campus two weeks later on a Friday morning for "Bible study". Twenty other girls come. Girls name bible study Delight. Delight girls cook dinner together, study the word together, serve hot chocolate to the homeless together, love on refugee kids together, stand for freedom together, wash cars together, and learn to live more like Christ together. Nine months later girls have grown from three to just under one hundred. The three girls are amazed and bewildered at all that God has done in and through Delight.

That is the quick and simple version of the story behind Delight. This story isn't necessarily unique and exciting. In fact, you've probably heard plenty of stories just like it. By this point, you may even be bored reading this story and e wondering why you bothered reading it in the first place.

HANG WITH US

What makes this story different is where the significance lies. You won't find it in the characters, or the setting, the climax, the dialogue, or even the theme. This story isn't actually about the story at all. It's about the author. An author that could take three sophomoric, average, and ordinary girls to write his own beautiful story through them. An Author that led unworthy and undeserving girls to start a Bible study that would eventually grow into a nation-wide ministry devoted to serving college women. This story is about the King of Kings and the Prince of Peace. God is the ultimate Author, the ultimate Bisionary, and the ultimate Dreamer. We are honored to be the characters in this story, but we are so thankful that we don't hold the pen in our hands. We leave the real story-writing to the greatest storyteller of all time.

MAY YOU HAVE THE POWER TO UNDERSTAND, AS ALL GOD'S PEOPLE SHOULD, HOW WIDE, HOW LONG, HOW HIGH AND HOW DEEP HIS LOVE IS.

EPHESIANS 3:18

DEAR FRIENDS,

As a ministry, we've been collecting stories from college women for well over three years now. In that amount of time we've read hundreds of stories, thousands of sentences, and hundreds of thousands of words all about how God is at work in the lives and hearts of women from all over the country. This book marks our 90th story published. We've probably read each of these stories well over ten times, meticulously looking for every misplaced comma, misspelled word, and edit that we could possibly find.

One might imagine that with the repetitious rhythm and the sheer volume of stories that flow through our email inboxes that these stories might start to lose some of their magic. *But we must say, quite the opposite has been true.*

Just a few months ago, I heard the infamous bleep signaling a new email on my phone as I was getting ready for bed one night. I opened the email intending to simply flag it to remind myself to edit it the next day at the office, but three minutes later I found myself engrossed in one of the early stages of a story from this very book.

There was nothing in this story out of the ordinary by worldly standards. Nothing blew up, nobody died, the world wasn't ending. To put it simply, it was a story of a college woman sharing how she encountered God's grace when she least expected it, when she didn't deserve it, and when she didn't even ask for it.

Right there in that moment, God reminded me of why we do what we do at Delight Ministries. We do it because everybody has a story like this. We all have pages and pages of God's grace winning every single time. Telling stories helps us realize that we serve a God who writes far better stories than we can ever fathom for ourselves.

So, even if the lightbulb hasn't switched for you yet, there will come a moment when you will reflect on your story and see right where God was at every twist and every turn. Our prayer is that the stories in this book are the catalyst for those lightbulb moments, the catalyst that wakes you up to the extravagance and simplicity of our God.

Mackenzie Baker + MacKenzie Wilson
Co-Founders of Delight Ministries

RACHEL H

RACHEL L

REGGIE

MADI

ANDREA

ERIN

BRIANNA

SHELBY

MORGAN

SYDNEY

FOREWORD

Telling our stories is the best way I know to discover God's abiding presence throughout all our days. Listening to each other's stories reveals the truth about our own lives. When the listening and the telling come together we begin to heal. In the healing many delightful things happen – hope, direction, love, joy.

Delight College Ministries invites women into a life-giving community experience where stories and truth lay a sweet foundation for soul refreshment and lasting friendships.

Robin Jones Gunn
Best-selling Author of Victim of Grace
and Spoken For

RACHEL H

UNIVERSITY OF ALABAMA
ELEMENTARY EDUCATION
SENIOR

Choosing Vulnerability

EXPERIENCING FREEDOM WHEN WE SHARE OUR BROKENNESS

"I do not belong here."

These were my first thoughts when I walked into a bible study I was interested in joining. It was spring of my junior year. A few months before I had rededicated my life to Christ, dropped my sorority, and attempted to find my place in a local mega church. The church encouraged us to join a small group where we would find accountability, vulnerability, and authentic relationships. After a few months debating whether or not I wanted to join one, I decided to look at the church group directory and try one out. I found one I thought I might like, and thought it wouldn't hurt to get to know a few girls. Fast forward a couple of weeks and there I was in a room of thirty other girls. It was hardly a "small" group. I walked in, debated turning around and leaving, and took a seat. As I looked around it seemed as though many of the girls already knew each other, they giggled, laughed, and commented on each other's cute shoes. I felt very intimidated and extremely out of place. As the night went on, the leaders introduced themselves, and everyone got to share where they were from and their major. I looked around and observed each girl, "perfect-Christian-good-girl" I thought, and about ten minutes into the "small" group I decided I would not be back.

I found myself a month later still attending the small group each Tuesday. I brought my Bible, sat, listened, put on a smile, and pretended like I was a "perfect-Christian-good-girl" like everyone else in the room, even though that was far from who I was. Each week was a different topic. We discussed bible verses, talked about our weeks, and occasionally someone would bring up something that was happening in their life. Sometimes I would want to speak but kept my mouth shut in fear of saying the wrong thing. I didn't want to be known as the newbie to the Christian walk. What if I said something wrong? Or worse, what if part of my past was exposed? I knew I didn't belong in that group, but I wanted to belong in that group. I wanted everyone to think I was holy and righteous and that I could fit into this "perfect-Christian-good-girl" small group.

"For all have sinned and fall short of the glory of God."
Romans 3:23

One Tuesday was different. We didn't discuss a Bible verse or talk about our weeks. "Tonight will be a little different." One of the leaders said. "I am going to share my testimony and then open the floor for anyone who wants to share theirs or share something they need freedom from." In a room of forty girls, Abby boldly and confidently shared her story. She shared how at a young age she was exposed to pornography and how that exposure became an addiction that followed her into her teenage years. She shared that she was not a "perfect Christian good-girl." She had a past but confidently explained that with God she overcame her addiction and temptation, and she was a new creation. Her past didn't define her. I admired her courage to expose her weakness and brokenness to all who looked up to her. She was open, honest, and her testimony of redemption was beautiful. I realized in that moment that this walk with Jesus isn't just for the "perfect Christian good-girls." It is for the sinners too. After all, we all are sinners, and we all have a broken story.

"Therefore, if anyone is in Christ, the new creation has come: The old has gone, the new is here!"
2 Corinthians 5:17

Her story ended, and the question was asked. Does anyone want to share? My heart started racing. Why did I feel an urge to speak up and share my brokenness? A million thoughts began to flood my mind. "What will these girls think when I tell them?" "You're finally friends with perfect-Christian-good-girls, don't ruin it, Rachel." My heart was beating so fast, my palms were getting sweaty, and then the words spilled out of my mouth. *"I'll share."*

"If we confess our sins, he is faithful and just and will forgive us our sins and purify us from all unrighteousness."
1 John 1:9

After a long awkward silence and stares around the room, I opened my mouth. There was no turning back. If God could redeem Abby's story, maybe He could redeem mine. So I shared. I shared how the events in my parents divorce made me feel unloved, unworthy, and unvalued. I shared how I searched for love and worth in all the wrong places, and now at twenty years old, I had given my heart and body away to many, many wrong relationships. I shared my abuse with drugs and alcohol and how it led me to depression and anxiety. I cried throughout the entire thing, and in the end, there was silence.

Did I share too much? Did I say the wrong things? What was everyone thinking? I immediately regretted my decision to share. My story had made it clear that I was not a "perfect-Christian-good-girl." I was certain that none of these girls could relate to me and was even more certain that they were all thinking the same thing. She does not belong here.

"Therefore confess your sins to each other and pray for each other so that you may be healed. The prayer of a righteous person is powerful and effective."
James 5:16

With my head down and my eyes filled, I felt hands gently start to touch my shoulders, girls started to surround me and Abby began to pray. Thirty women, all together were now praying for my freedom and healing. It was a messy, tear filled, beautiful moment of freedom. As the prayer went on my heavy sobbing went to soft whimpers, to an overwhelming peaceful relaxation. I was exposed, I was fully known, and yet I was completely at peace with myself, with others, and with God.

What I thought would be a moment of complete judgment by others became a moment of healing, restoration, and growth. Not only for myself, but for others in the room as well. After I shared, girl after girl came forward, spoke up and shared her story, her struggle, her brokenness. A girl would share, we would gather, pray, and cry. Another girl would share, we would gather, pray, and cry some more. We shared into the late hours of the night, and I remember driving home listening to worship music, crying, and praising the Lord for the goodness we had experienced.

There is true beauty in being broken before the Lord. As women in Christ, we often feel obligated to put on this pretty face, perfect hair, perfect outfit, wonder woman appearance. But could it be that Jesus meets us most in our messiest moments? He makes us radiant and beautiful in the midst of our brokenness. He heals our hearts as we become exposed. And as we are shattering our image and pride, He is picking up the pieces and creating something worthy. These broken, messy moments are the moments when we truly feel Him, meet Him, and know Him. For me, in that moment of complete vulnerability and exposure, that is where I met the fullness of His truth, promises, and glory. His presence was right next to me, and I felt Him whisper, you are known, you are loved, and you are forgiven.

"My grace is sufficient for you, for my power is made perfect in weakness." Therefore I will boast all the more gladly about my weaknesses, so that Christ's power may rest on me."
2 Corinthians 12:9

The Gospel is beautiful, but it is messy. Yes, Jesus came down and out of unexplainable love died on a cross for our sins. But in the moment of the crucifixion it was anything but beautiful. He was betrayed, whipped, beaten, mocked, and hurt. His hands were nailed, and His blood poured out. The plan of accusation was scandalous, and if we truly think about everything that went down leading up to Jesus at the cross, it is almost hard to imagine. The beauty however is that after the mess came the glory. After the pain came the victory. After the hurt came the healing. Likewise, after I shared my sins, I found forgiveness. After I shared my pain, I became whole again. This is a heavenly promise; There is always beauty after brokenness. The Bible says that His power is made perfect in our weakness. It is not made perfect when we run around and serve in five different campus ministries. It is not made perfect when we post an encouraging Bible verse on Instagram. No, it is made perfect in when we are weak, broken, and our sins are exposed. It is made perfect when we are in need of a Savior to put us back together and make us whole.

"Whoever conceals their sins does not prosper, but the one who confesses and renounces them finds mercy."
Proverbs 28:13

Why is it so much easier to hide our sins and struggles rather than expose them? We have learned from the first story in the Bible that after Adam and Eve ate the forbidden fruit they hid from God. He came searching for them in the garden, and they ran to hide— broken and ashamed. It was only when Adam and Eve came out from hiding, exposed their nakedness and their new sinful heart, did God meet them, clothe them, and ultimately create a story of redemption to restore them. It is easy to hide and hard to confess. There is no doubt about this truth about our humanly flesh. As hard as it is to do, we need to be authentic, vulnerable, and real with those around us. Life will always have struggles, and we will always need guidance. The healing and restoration of Jesus only comes when we are open and honest. This can be a challenging thing for many of us to do. However, the beauty happens when we come out of hiding and expose our struggles, pain, and sins. We become exposed, but we become known by God. We become broken, but we become healed by His blood. We become messy, but by Him, we become clean, whole and new.

It was clear that the Lord had done a beautiful work in each of our hearts that night. The "perfect-Christian-good-girl" image I had of others was torn down and replaced with the authentic friendships I was promised I would find. Many girls reached out to me after I shared that night and told me how my story was similar to theirs and how they struggled with many of the same things. Some of us even came up with ways that we could keep each other accountable. What once felt like a place where I had to pretend to be holy and righteous to fit in was now a place where I was accepted for my past and encouraged for my future. I belonged. It was truly comforting to know that I was not alone in my pain and weakness. The enemy would want nothing more for us to hide our sins, hide our shame, and never fully experience the whole power and whole freedom that comes with vulnerability and exposure. But we can rest on the promise, that through Jesus alone, power is made perfect in weakness, and brokenness is always made beautiful.

KEY VERSES:
Romans 3:23
2 Corinthians 5:17
1 John 1:9
James 5:16
2 Corinthians 12:9
Proverbs 28:13

DISCUSSION QUESTIONS:
+ Has there ever been a time in your life when you felt like you didn't belong? What caused you to feel out of place?
+ Do you ever feel obligated to put on a pretty face, perfect hair, perfect outfit, perfect Christian appearance? If so, why do you feel pressured to put on this facade? Why is perfectionism often glorified in today's Christian culture?
+ Why is it that some things are often times easy to hide, but hard to confess? What makes you fear vulnerability? Are you scared of saying the wrong thing, not being accepted, your past being exposed, etc.?
+ Rachel explains that when she chose to be vulnerable before her community she found new freedom in Christ. Is there something you've been too afraid to share? What might you be missing if you choose to keep this to yourself?
+ When we choose to share vulnerably, we become exposed, but we become known by God. We become broken, but we become healed by His blood. We become messy, but by Him, we become clean, whole, and new. How does choosing to be vulnerable strengthen our relationship with God? How do you already see Jesus making your brokenness beautiful?

DEVOTIONALS

CONTRIBUTOR: *Katie Knell*

DAY 1

As we enter into our walk as a disciple of Christ, we often find a tension that can only be attributed to one transformed truth: we are no longer citizens of this broken, fallen world, but we have been made new and counted as a heavenly citizen. By denying our past, we seek renewed hope for what's ahead in abandoning our all for Jesus' name.

While this newfound identity promises freedom and newfound hope, often times we are left disillusioned when we are ostracized and rejected. Does this not sound familiar to the story of the one whom we are following? Despite the parallel, we often are left unsettled and questioning, "Will He provide in this transition? What will my relationships consist of? Should I turn back now?"

Within community, God created you to be relished and known while also being revealed and raw. In our pride and deception of what others may perceive, we often do not choose to voluntarily admit our waywardness to those around us. New phases can often leave us feeling uncomfortable, unknown, and wildly insecure. While these emotions are valid, we also must consider what is holding us back.

Reflect on a time when you were entering into a new season. Consider the instability and adjustments you saw happening around you. Consider the growth amidst the pain and consider the unsettledness that led you to deeper understanding of both yourself and the Lord.

KEY VERSES:
"For all have sinned and fall short of the glory of God."
Romans 3:23

"Again, truly I tell you that if two of you on earth agree about anything they ask for, it will be done for them by my Father in heaven."

Matthew 18:19

REFLECTION QUESTIONS:
+ Has there ever been a time in your life when you felt like you didn't belong? What caused you to feel out of place?

DAY 2

No one wants to admit they aren't perfect, and we certainly don't want to address that we fall short...Every.Single.Day. We are bound to a culture that not only encourages but expects the perfect balance in every aspect of your world. We must compete for the perfect body, relationships, and work-life balance while also never addressing that this feat is nearly impossible. Something has to give.

It is quite literally counter-cultural to admit our frailties and to seek vulnerability in relationships in fear of turning another away by our "weaknesses". But, what if it was truly our brokenness that set us apart and revealed a glory beyond our own? As believers, we set to live a life just like this, abandoning the misconception that we must aim for perfection. The key? Progress over perfection.

KEY VERSES:
"Therefore, if anyone is in Christ, the new creation has come: The old has gone, the new is here!"
2 Corinthians 5:17

"Therefore confess your sins to each other and pray for each other so that you may be healed. The prayer of a righteous person is powerful and effective."
James 5:16

REFLECTION QUESTIONS:
+ Why is it that some things are often times easy to hide but hard to confess? What makes you fear vulnerability? Are you scared of saying the wrong thing, not being accepted, your past being exposed, etc?

Often times, our disillusionment of our worth in Christ directly parallels our knowledge and true understanding of the gospel. For many, we have heard the story of Jesus' time on earth – the healing of the blind, the wedding where water was turned to wine, and Jesus' association with prostitutes and more—while others are walking through learning who this God is for the very first time. Wherever you may fit in your understanding of this journey, what are some of the facets you struggle to accept about the Gospel? What hindrances do you find within your own heart that leave you unable to accept your worth and therefore boldly share with others the good news of the Gospel?

Consider this: if Jesus' earthly mission was to only associate with the elite, picture the Pharisees here, what hope would it bring for those that saw the reality of their sins in their every day lives? Just as Rachel notes the picture of the "perfect-Christian-good-girl", we soon begin to see the irony of it all, that personas aside, we all have fallen short, but it is by grace that we have been saved. Take heart today, sisters. He did not come for the haughty but for the humble.

KEY VERSES:
"Whoever conceals their sins does not prosper, but the one who confesses and renounces them finds mercy."
Proverbs 28:13

"I have not come to call the righteous, but sinners to repentance."
Luke 5:32

REFLECTION QUESTIONS:
+ Do you ever feel obligated to put on a *pretty face, perfect hair, perfect outfit, perfect Christian appearance*? If so, why do you feel pressured to put on this facade? Why is perfectionism often glorified in today's Christian culture?

DAY 4

Living in a sinful, fallen world, we are constantly bombarded with the expectation that we must appear to have our lives in order. We are told that if we act by our own strength, we will recognize that we do not need the assistance of someone else. Often times, we are left fragile and lonely as our attempts to upkeep this façade is challenging. It is not until we are convicted by the mighty work of the Holy Spirit that we address our need for a Savior and accept that true transformation arises from inward out.

Getting to a place that allows you to speak freely and vulnerably of your hurts and your past require elements of both grace and courage, two of which we cannot muster up by our own strength. Specifically, we see how Rachel struggled to share her heart amidst a large group of young women, until she began to witness the Spirit move in Abby's and then later her own.

Often times, we are blinded by the pride and insecurity of admitting what appears to make us look "weak". BUT, that is the beauty in it all…that when we are bent low, in a posture of humility, Christ desires to make His glory known in and through us. What greater gift and lightest yoke to carry in His name! How will you lead in sharing your story today?

KEY VERSES:
"Then the man and his wife heard the sound of the Lord God as he was walking in the garden in the cool of the day, and they hid from the Lord God among the trees of the garden. But the Lord God called to the man, "Where are you"?
Genesis 3:8-9

"You have searched me, Lord, and you know me. You know when I sit and when I rise; you perceive my thoughts from afar…you are familiar with all my ways. Before a word is on my tongue you, Lord, know it completely."
Psalm 139:1-4

REFLECTION QUESTIONS:

+ Rachel explains that when she chose to be vulnerable before her community she found new freedom in Christ. Is there something you've been too afraid to share? What might you be missing if you choose to keep this to yourself?

+ When we choose to share vulnerably we become exposed, but we become known by God. We become broken, but we become healed by His blood. We become messy, but by Him, we become clean, whole, and new. How does choosing to be vulnerable strengthen our relationship with God? How do you already see Jesus making your brokenness beautiful?

RACHEL L

UNC WILMINGTON
INTERNATIONAL STUDIES
JUNIOR

Trusting His Story

LETTING GOD HOLD THE PEN

My parents got a divorce my senior year and the only way I knew
how to cope was to become a control freak. Not necessarily of my
surroundings but more so in my mind and in my heart. I decided to take
up the control to write my own narrative because I wasn't going to let
my story end up like my parents.

I found my freshman year roommate on Facebook. I was scrolling
through the UNCW Class of 2017 page and found a picture of a girl that
looked a lot cooler and athletic than me, so I clicked on her page and
messaged her.

We met at a Texas Roadhouse half-way between our two home towns
after having in depth-conversations on Facebook with questions like,
"What's your favorite color?" "Any food allergies?" Okay not that one but
still you get the point. SO much cheesiness! After dinner, we awkwardly
hugged and said "So . . . roommates?" and the rest was history.

I was sitting in one of the computer labs in our high school mindlessly
exploring hotnewhiphop.com, seeing if Drizzy dropped any new fire
tracks when I saw an email pop up. It was from UNCW and the headline
said: ROOM ASSIGNMENT. I clicked on it ever so gracefully to read the
dreaded words: GALLOWAY.

"Really Jesus?" I thought, "The party dorm? You know my past! You
know I struggle with letting it go a little too far with guys. You know I
like to take shots in closets so no one knows I'm drunk but me! How are
you going to put me in the party dorm?"

Then the tears came.

That is the first time in my life that I, truly to my core, believed Jesus failed me as a daughter. I believed His plans for my story wasn't a good enough narrative than the one I could write for myself, and I felt I was better off with the pencil in my hand. It was the first time I realized I believed that I knew what I needed more than Him.

It makes me think of the time when Jesus asked Peter to walk out on the water towards him. Peter stepped out of the boat, but the second he took his eyes off Jesus and looked at the waves, he began to sink.

Sounds a lot like our lives. We'll muster up enough faith to step out of the boat, but once we look at the waves, the pains of this life, we don't trust Jesus enough to keep going, so we sink.

You know how Jesus responded to Peter? Jesus catches Him and says, "Why did you doubt?"

Being placed in Galloway definitely, to me, felt like Jesus calling me out amongst the waves to trust Him. I didn't understand why he would send me into a place that could easily cause me to stumble or to feel the vulnerability of my past. I was frustrated. I was angry, and I doubted that He would help me walk out on the water. But, to my surprise, His hand wasn't as far a reach as I had thought.

"Immediately Jesus reached out his hand and caught him. "You of little faith," he said, "why did you doubt?"'
Matthew 14:31

The first day I walked in to Galloway all I noticed was an insanely tiny room that I was sure would be impossible to live in. I also noticed my roommate, Jordyn, and I's plethora of moving boxes that took up every square inch of our room.

"This is what my life has come to," I thought, "living in a 16ft x 10ft room with a bright color loving, Athletic Barbie"

I didn't speak to anyone that day really. I sat in my bed and wept. I wept because I said goodbye to my family, and I wept because I was on a hall with 72 other people and felt all alone. I wasn't supposed to feel this way. I wasn't supposed to be alone. I had spent my entire senior year mourning losing my mother to another man, and I thought I had suffered through enough loneliness. But that is something that the Lord has so graciously taught me over the years, He never promised that I wouldn't be lonely. He just promised I wouldn't be alone.

And so it began... my journey in Galloway. That night I stayed up writing a blog post about how doomed humanity was without Jesus and how college was not a fit for me. Oh, how wrong I was.

On UNCW's campus, I lived on the 6th floor of Galloway Hall. We called ourselves G6 (and a bunch of other punny nick-names).

I wish there was a way to put into words the way my heart felt when I looked at each and every person that lived on my hall. I wish there was a way to accurately describe each and every person that lived on this floor, and I deeply wish there was a way to eloquently tell the stories of each unique and purpose-filled person that I have met, right there on the 6th floor of Galloway

It would be impossible to tell the story of 72 different people and be able to accurately asses what their lives have looked like in the past and what they look like now, but fortunately for me (someone who loves to write about redemption, triumph, and love), I was able to find something that all 72 of us had in common— and will have in common— forever.

And the common ground we share is this: we all long to know that we are worthy of pursuit, worthy of someone that will truly know us, truly love us, and look at us for who we are and still stick around.

Isn't that what we all yearn for?
To know that we are worth it?

There was not a day in Galloway that went by that I didn't fall in love over and over again with the people I met. Each story was so unique; each story so different.

Our floor was filled with blondes, brunettes, freckles, long hair, short hair, tan skin, pale skin, blue eyes, brown eyes. Our floor was filled with laughter, tears, loud voices, obnoxious hall sports, an abundance of perfume or axe body spray, and hundreds of other unique compilations that you would easily find in a freshman dorm.

Over a period of two semesters, 10 months, 43 weeks, 304 days, I fell in love with each and every hug, smile, and laugh on my floor, and I went from feeling like the loneliest girl in the world to feeling like the most loved and cherished person around.

I saw each person on my floor through the eyes of their Maker, and that is what made them all so beautiful to me.

I saw life in places that were really, really dark. Instead of looking at brokenness as a terrible illness, I looked at it as a beautiful sign that God is good and ever present, and He is fighting for us in a world that is out to ruin our hearts.

Jesus taught me a lot about myself in my freshman year of college. I learned a lot about timidity, boldness, and strength. I learned that I couldn't say no to the world unless I let Jesus lead me to my knees.

I learned that I selfishly loved myself, was still full of vain conceit, and my life, as much as I wish it didn't, revolved around a heart that denied what Jesus wanted for me. But what I have learned most of all is that it is OK. It's OK to be broken. It's OK to hurt. It's OK to be lonely. It's OK to be frustrated. It's OK to cry. . . but it's not OK to think that we are better off writing the end of our story.

Through all of this Jesus gave me clear eyes to see right into my own heart, to see right into my own pain, and to see how intricately He had been walking throughout my own story. He didn't leave me behind to figure out all of the right answers; instead, He showed me that even when I didn't feel like He was near, He was always hidden in the details. I began to see the uniqueness in every story that He was writing for the people on my dorm hall, and it made me take a step back and realize that I didn't have to have it all figured out. I didn't have to know what was coming next, and my story would be just as beautiful whether or not I knew what was on the next page.

Looking back now, I believe this is a time where Jesus could interject and say: "You of little faith. Why did you doubt?"

I have countless books sitting on my desk right now that I have read half-way through and then given up on the ending. I'll read what's comfortable. I'll read the parts that fill my heart with wonder, but once

I read something that challenges me or alludes that I must jump into the deep, I shut the book. I keep the ending open because I fear the unknown, I fear the leap from one piece of literature to the other because I am so set on what I have so deeply cherished within the first novel.

It all comes down to the fact that I don't trust that Jesus is a better author of the ending of my story than me. I want to be in control. I want to have the final say in who I am and where I end up, but I forget that the day I decided to follow Jesus, I gave up that control. I so often want to grab the pencil from Jesus, but the reality of this is that at the end of whatever story you are currently writing with your life, Jesus is a much better author.

When you say yes to Jesus, you say no to being the author of your story, and you say yes to Him being the hero.

"Being confident of this, that he who began a good work in you will carry it on to completion until the day of Christ Jesus."
Philippians 1:6

We can rest in the fact that Jesus, the Author and Perfector of our faith, knows the ending. He wrote the ending of our story long before we were even formed. Why are we able to trust Jesus in this? Because He, the King of Kings, left His throne in Heaven, so that you wouldn't have to worry or be anxious about the ending.

Sometimes we have to look at whatever situation we are facing and say, "OK God, even though this hurts and even though I don't understand, I trust you enough to walk away because You promise me that you will not let me go back to where I've been."

Maybe this is what Jesus means when He says to pick up our cross? Maybe picking up our cross isn't a one-time deal. Maybe it is daily, in the mundane, in the every day choices that we make. To see the beauty of the cross and choose its power over our lives every day instead of letting our pasts permeate our mindsets and hold us back in what "could've" or "should've" been.

"Forget the former things; do not dwell on the past. See, I am doing a new thing! Now it springs up; do you not perceive it? I am making a way in the wilderness and streams in the wasteland."
Isaiah 43:18-19

"Be still before the Lord and wait patiently for him; do not fret when people succeed in their ways, when they carry out their wicked schemes."
Psalm 37:7

It has been three years since I have lived on G6. I rarely walk over to that side of campus anymore, but the other day, I happened to walk passed Galloway on my way to the dining hall. Who would have thought that the place, which I believed was going to produce so much pain and rebellion within me, was actually the place that Christ would use to heal me. The Lord restored life within me that year when He showed me the way He intricately loved everyone in that hallway, including me.

He is the Restorer of hope, when all else seems lost. He is the Redeemer of stories when we feel like we deserve to be written off, and He is the Author of life, even when we are tempted to take control of the pen.

"Now to him who is able to do immeasurably more than all we ask or imagine, according to his power that is at work within us."
Ephesians 3:20

I would've never chosen where I am right now for myself, but I know I am exactly where He wants me. The funny thing is, I feel like looking back it was never me writing my story in the first place. He knew all along what I needed, and like a good Father, He fiercely protected the destiny He says is rightfully mine. Not because of anything that I have done or will ever do but because of what He did that beautiful day on the Cross of Calvary.

It doesn't matter who is trying to write your narrative—you, your family, your friends, or any other relationship that you are in. The reality is He is a better author, and He is faithful in giving us beauty for our ashes.

KEY VERSES:
Matthew 14:31
Philippians 1:6
Isaiah 43:18-19
Psalm 37:7
Ephesians 3:20

DISCUSSION QUESTIONS:

+ What is your need for control rooted in? Is it fear of failure, rejection, loneliness, ending up like your parents, etc.?

+ Rachel shares how when you say yes to Jesus, you say no to being the author of your story, and you say yes to Him being the hero. Does your life proclaim this statement? What are the areas in your life that you still want to be the hero of? Why?

+ So often we enter into situations with confidence and excitement for God's plans, but the moment we face hardships we lose all trust. How can we remain steadfast with our eyes on Jesus even when we feel overwhelmed by our circumstances?

+ In the last few months, think back on a moment where you felt like the Lord's plan for your story wasn't as good as the one you could write for yourself. Looking at it today, how have you already begun to see His purpose unfold?

+ Are you fixating on the big picture and missing what God is doing in the details? How does being present in the in-between and the little moments allow us to trust God as the Author of our story? Instead of worrying about what's on the next page, how can you be confident in what He's already written?

DEVOTIONALS

DEVOTIONAL CONTRIBUTOR: *Katie Sura*

DAY 1

The reality is that having control feels good. If you have ever been in a place or position that holds the reigns in some aspect, you know it is true. In a place of control, we are able to call the shots, anticipate and avoid discomfort and pain, and ultimately get what we want. Naturally, then, our reaction would be to strive to gain control over our lives and the idea of stepping down from the position of authority in calling the shots sounds foolish. In a world that is constantly attempting to convince us that we are the center of our own universe, the thought of surrendering power seems completely absurd. But when did Jesus ever emulate a life that reflected the patterns of the world? Written within the New Testament, Jesus' life reveals a conscious decision to surrender control when He chose to step down from His throne and live a servant life, ultimately leading to His own crucifixion. But the story doesn't stop there. In Jesus' death and resurrection, we are able to see the trustworthy hand of the Father who is in the unshakeable habit of restoring life. He cannot help but bring what was broken to wholeness and what was dead back to life. Our Father thrives off of ushering timely beauty into of the most hopeless of circumstances and teaching feet to dance on frustration. True, the concept of surrendering control is backwards from what the world says, but in choosing to allow God to hold the pen in authoring our stories, we say yes to a life guided by the most perfect Leader who promises to lead us in the path of life. He was, is, and always will be the hero of the story; we are simply called to follow His lead.

KEY VERSES:
"You make known to me the path of life; you will fill me with joy in your presence, with eternal pleasures at your right hand."
Psalm 16:11

"In their hearts humans plan their course, but the LORD establishes their steps."
Proverbs 16:9

REFLECTION QUESTIONS:

+ What is your need for control rooted in? Is it fear of failure, rejection, loneliness, ending up like your parents, etc.?

+ Rachel shares how when you say yes to Jesus, you say no to being the author of your story, and you say yes to Him being the hero. Does your life proclaim this statement? What are the areas in your life that you still want to be the hero of? Why?

DAY 2

We live in a world that thrives off of highlight reels. Think about it. Instagram, Snapchat, Facebook, Twitter, Pinterest. Most of us can barely sit at a red stop light for more than a few seconds without reaching for our phones to pull up the latest posts. Although we probably all recognize that our own lives are not constantly filled with "post worthy moments," we cannot help but be influenced with the underlying expectation that our everyday should look like cloud 9, free of struggles, pain, and anything that brings discomfort. It is rare, however, that life ends up meeting all of our expectations; this even includes situations and seasons that Jesus calls us in to. So how do we remain grounded when life does not meet our expectations but instead seems to continually throw us hardships that we cannot avoid? We must look at our foundation and daily refuse to have our grounding found in anything but Jesus. When life turns out to be less than ideal, ever-constant Truth and Love will keep our feet steady, consistently reminding us of who we are in Christ. Expectations of having satisfaction through a highlight-filled life will only produce a weak foundation, but by daily choosing Truth to act as our base, we can experience the beauty of replacing our strict expectations of how life should look with a heart of expectancy, knowing the faithful Author who deeply loves His children will never stop leading us from glory to glory.

KEY VERSES:
"Being confident of this, that he who began a good work in you will carry it on to completion until the day of Christ Jesus."
Philippians 1:6

REFLECTION QUESTIONS:
+ So often we enter into situations with confidence and excitement for God's plans, but the moment we face hardships we lose all trust. How can we remain steadfast with our eyes on Jesus even when we feel overwhelmed by our circumstances?

DAY 3

Do you ever find yourself wishing there was a personalized script of your life that could offer assurance of how everything will play out, rather than having to navigate the unknown? Or find yourself attempting to manipulate situations in order to receive an outcome that you can predict? Life would be much easier if we knew how everything was going to turn out. But in these moments of wishing we knew the end result, we forget our position in the story as the finite, loved creation, not the infinite, loving Creator. Scripture reveals that God rarely works according to man's requests and plans, but instead He invites His beloved into situations that involve stepping out of comfort and into a place that requires His strength and grace to be the heartbeat of the journey. By reflecting on stories woven throughout the narrative of Scripture, we are able to see the confident, faithful hand of the Father guiding His people in methods of glory and redemption. Abraham, Esther, Moses, David, Job, Paul. These accounts and so many more offer a glimpse into the lives of God's people, who similarly to us, did not know the outcome of their stories but accepted the chance to be led by grace and allowed the most perfect Author to hold control. By taking 2 Corinthians 2:19 to heart, we become free to follow a very intentional Father who adores writing intimate stories of beauty and invites His strength to shoulder our weaknesses. He always has our best in mind and refuses to leave us unattended in our own narratives. Remember who you are and who He is and surrender control to the only One who is worthy to hold the position as Leader.

KEY VERSES:
"But he said to me, "My grace is sufficient for you, for my power is made perfect in weakness." Therefore I will boast all the more gladly about my weaknesses, so that Christ's power may rest on me."
2 Corinthians 12:9

REFLECTION QUESTIONS:
+ In the last few months, think back on a moment where you felt like the Lord's plan for your story wasn't as good as the one you could write for yourself. Looking at it today, how have you already begun to see His purpose unfold?

DAY 4

The future is a topic that can hold a broad scope of emotions from anxiety to anticipation, excitement to fear. When thinking about the future, it is easy to get caught up in wishing we were someplace else or making a step-by-step plan that will end in achieving a desired addition to our lives. We are mentally taken out of our present reality, and our minds are filled with thoughts such as "Once I have that then..." or "I will be okay when..." The truth is that all we have is today; we do not know what tomorrow will hold. However, a greater truth remains: Christ came and conquered death, securing the promise of hope, redemption, and life. The end of the story is a guarantee. This enables us to presently walk in freedom, knowing that we are a part of the most triumphant story of greatest love. Rather than existing under the pressure of planning our lives, we are able to wake up each morning and let Jesus remind us of who we are in Him; we are His beloved. The stress of micromanaging each second of our lives is off. By remembering that our core identity stems from the perfect love of the Father, our eyes are opened to the realness of His presence in our day to day. We are able to live out of victory, knowing that the One who holds the pen in writing our story will never leave us on our own but promises to walk with us every step of the way. He always has our best interest in mind, providing a firm foundation of Truth when we fall down and offering His strength to carry us when we are weak. Let Him author your story; let Him lead you into glory, for truly, the best is yet to come.

KEY VERSES:
"Be still before the Lord and wait patiently for him; do not fret when people succeed in their ways, when they carry out their wicked schemes."
Psalm 37:7

"He who was seated on the throne said, "I am making everything new!" Then he said, 'Write this down, for these words are trustworthy and true.'"
Revelation 21:5

REFLECTION QUESTIONS:
+ Are you fixating on the big picture and missing what God is doing in the details? How does being present in the in-between and the little moments allow us to trust God as the Author of our story? Instead of worrying about what's on the next page, how can you be confident in what He's already written?

BRIANNA

PEPPERDINE UNIVERSITY
PSYCHOLOGY
JUNIOR

Joyfully Obedient

DRAWING CLOSER TO THE LORD THROUGH OBEDIENCE

I love quizzes and tests. Not academic tests, definitely not academic tests, but ones that are meant to suggest career paths, personality tests, and how familiar am I with Harry Potter. Personality tests are my favorite, and this may have to do with the fact that I am a psychology major who loves knowing people to their core – or at least try to. I love how every person really is unique and seeing others as individuals participating, or not participating, in society.

I've always loved being unique. The greatest compliment a person could ever give me is that I am unlike anyone they had ever met before. I never wanted to conform, and I was never concerned with following the crowd. When all the girls were out playing with dolls, I was acting out Star Wars with the neighborhood boys. When people were going to the movies every weekend, I would spend my nights devouring books and spending time with family. In high school, I fell in love with Jesus and pressed into faith, serving as a leader at the Christian club on campus and going to worship nights rather than parties. As I went into Pepperdine, I knew that I wanted to stand out and to have an experience that differed from everyone else's. You could say that I fell in love with individualism and had made an idol out of the idea.

I took pride in who God made me to be and firmly believed that I was able to tackle this faith thing myself. Despite prompting from the Spirit to join a community, I started college with the mindset that I was a strong individual who could bear all things on my shoulders.

"Then the LORD God said, 'It is not good that man should be alone."
Genesis 2:18a

But you see the thing is, even from the beginning, God did not intend for us to go through life alone. He did not intend for us to bear all things as a way of flexing our so-called spiritual muscles. God was teaching me this lesson throughout the entirety of my college experience, but it culminated in the beginning of the second semester of my junior year.

My parents would say that my independence peaked while I studied in Argentina my sophomore year. The gypsy lifestyle gave me a reason to not get plugged into a church while abroad or even to call home all that often. If you scrolled through my social media, I was the girl that experienced multiple cultures, visited exotic places, a friend to many, and I was in love. The constant buzz of excitement drowned out the loneliness of the lifestyle. But the buzz wears off, and the buzz does not provide the comfort and satisfaction that relationships with other individuals do. As the excitement wore away, I found myself wanting to go to a familiar coffee shop with a friend who understood me rather than struggling with a language barrier while chasing down the thrill. I felt God's nudge to join a community, to really join a group of people and bare my struggles, joys, and ugliness to other followers of Christ. However, life at that point was full of the unknown and transition. I used this to tune out His voice, not wanting to give up this strong independent image I had built for myself. The rest of my walk was thriving– I was growing exponentially in my knowledge of Scripture and diligence in prayer, but there was a section of me that did not want to give it all up to Christ, to be obedient to His call to be in community. Being in community with other believers meant giving up my autonomy. *"No way!"* I thought, *"That would make me miserable."*

I came back from my year abroad. Life became chaotic: friends and I were overcommitted, my best friend abruptly left for long term mission in Mexico, my relationship ended, things were tough. But I had developed an image for myself that I could not seem to break no matter how much God pushed me to let go of some of my independence to allow others in and help me. When I was wrapped up in the ups and downs of life, I did not have a community to encourage me to persevere, to lean on when I could no longer carry all my burdens, or to rejoice with when all was good. This period of loneliness was not easy, and it was definitely not something I asked for. At times, I felt frustrated that nobody seemed to rally around me and distant from the Creator because of the lack of human support. I did not understand the loneliness. I was doing all the right things and attending all the right events, but I still felt as though I had been abandoned.

God's voice surrounding community continually got louder, and I could no longer drown it out with a busy schedule, a shallow faith, or a false sense of community. Weekly announcements about small groups at church pervaded my thoughts.

"Alright alright, Jesus. I will try this and listen to this command to submit to the body, but please do not make me give up my autonomy to mold to a stereotype."

After just one night of attending a small group, I fell in love with the most eclectic group of individuals that exuded warmth and encouraged me more than I'd ever been encouraged before. All in only two hours. They rejoiced, wept, and danced together in life. They knew the beauty and the ugly of each individual. At the second small group I went to, every person shared about where they were in their walk with Christ. After sharing, everyone was genuinely supportive and praying for each individual. Even after the night ended, I would get text messages from people who barely knew me asking how they could pray for me and asking specific questions about information I had shared. They listened, they cared, and they were constantly praying. My eyes opened to the truth of community and God's desire for us to live together. God's call on my life to live in community was not a call to conform to a standard but to live in unity with a diverse group of believers. Think about how this world is designed. We are designed to live in family from birth and that's what these people were. They were a family—a messy, broken, wonderful group of people— and I finally accepted God's invitation to obey His design of living as one body under one Father.

"How good and pleasant it is when God's people live together in unity!"
Psalm 133:1

"And let us consider how we may spur one another on toward love and good deeds, not giving up meeting together, as some are in the habit of doing, but encouraging one another—and all the more as you see the Day approaching."
Hebrews 10: 24-25

Shortly after stepping into community, God revealed to me that obedience to His commands, whether it be community, chastity, service, was meant to bring me ultimate joy in drawing closer to His being. In short, obedience to God is not meant to be a killjoy but to lead us to ultimate joy. He has been a Father for quite some time. He knows the inner workings of our hearts, shouldn't we trust Him with our joy? For me, the idolatry of individualism led to the resistance towards participating in the body and committing to it as one of its members. I valued my autonomy over His church, and it led to months of loneliness and dissatisfaction. After obeying His command to take part in the body, I experienced joy, and even better than experiencing it alone, I get to experience joy with a stellar group of people I now call family who encourage me daily through Scripture, prayer, and the occasional dance session. Even though I began to become involved in a group, I did not lose my individuality. Scripture points to the necessity of each part of the body of Christ. If every person were the same, the body would not advance. Diversity is needed for growth and community is not a group of identical individuals but a diverse group working towards the same purpose.

"Moreover, we have all had human fathers who disciplined us and we respected them for it. How much more should we submit to the Father of spirits and live! They disciplined us for a little while as they thought best; but God disciplines us for our good, in order that we may share in his holiness. No discipline seems pleasant at the time, but painful. Later on, however, it produces a harvest of righteousness and peace for those who have been trained by it."
Hebrews 12:9-11

Though discipline and obedience may not come easily, the Spirit gives us the ability to follow Christ's example if we ask for it. It is not always enjoyable in the moment but benefits our being in the long term as He uses it to draw us nearer to His holiness. It all happens, God desires it for us because of His love demonstrated to us through the cross and resurrection. God does not sit in this mighty throne and look down with contempt on His people. He does not plot ways to make us miserable. Instead, God left His throne to suffer for His children out of sacrificial love—agape. When the realization of how great His love is for us, it makes it easier to obey Him and His Word, to give up things that may bring us instant gratification for the ultimate joy found in Christ. So really, what is stopping us from dropping everything and obeying Christ with all our being? Joy awaits us in His arms.

"But now that you have been set free from sin and have become slaves of God, the benefit you reap leads to holiness, and the result is eternal life. For the wages of sin is death, but the gift of God is eternal life in Christ Jesus our Lord."
Romans 6:22-23

KEY VERSES:
Genesis 2:18a
Psalm 133:1
Hebrews 10:24-25
Hebrews 12:9-11
Romans 6:22-23

DISCUSSION QUESTIONS:
+ Coming to college, did you desire to stand out or be an individual? What did you want to be noticed for?
+ Brianna got so caught up in chasing after an image of individuality and independence that in the end left her feeling isolated and alone. Can you think of a time in your life where you fought for a certain identity? How does fighting for an identity outside of Christ leave us feeling?
+ Why is it so important to surround yourself with community? How does the support of a Christ-centered community strengthen you faith and increase your growth? Is community something you need to start making a priority?
+ How can you begin to let go of your self-focused mindset and instead, walk in obedience for the Lord? Have you been missing something that the Lord has been telling you because you've been so concerned with yourself? What might obedience for the Lord look like in your life right now?
+ For most of us growing up, obedience had a negative connotation when it came to curfews and report cards, but how does obedience to God look different? How can you see obedience as a joyful effort in drawing closer to Him, rather than a set of rules to follow? Do you have faith that the Lord has a greater plan in mind when you choose to be obedient?

DEVOTIONALS

DAY 1

We all have that one thing that makes us unique. Maybe we come from a big family? Or are from a small town. We love dogs, or we are athletic. Sometimes the ways we identify ourselves start to define us and it can be scary and vulnerable to let go of the people we have created. Let's start with social media. We have created a brand that we must remain loyal to . . . only posting once a week, all black and whites? Clever captions and perfect VSCO filters. This week, take note of the things that build you up and tear you down. Do you live and die on the approval of the people around you? Are you putting too much stake in how the world defines you to be or do you quiet the voices around you with the words of our Creator? How do you cope? When you're bored, what do you do to occupy your mind? Be present and aware of the food you are feeding your mind. Try deleting your social media app for the week and watch what God does when you quiet the voices that tell you that you are anything but worthy and loved.

KEY VERSES:
"Finally, brothers and sisters, whatever is true, whatever is noble, whatever is right, whatever is pure, whatever is lovely, whatever is admirable—if anything is excellent or praiseworthy—think about such things."
Philippians 4:8

REFLECTION QUESTIONS:
+ Coming to college, did you desire to stand out or be an individual? What did you want to be noticed for?

DAY 2

Brianna explains how torn she was between the identity she created and the person God was calling her to be. It is so crucial to learn from Brianna's story and understand that any identity apart from Christ is enslaving. For months, she felt the tug on her heart for community, but because she had created this image of being free-spirited and independent, she became imprisoned. So did the "free-spirit" in her because an exhausting game of lying to herself and saying no to God. This is a really heavy way to live. God's heart for His children is freedom, joy, peace, love, and self-expression. The community Brianna felt called to really is humbling. As much as community can be encouragement and celebration, it is growth and challenge. You can get away with a lot more when no one is watching. But community also means accountability. Is God calling you to something that means letting go of something you hold dear? Sometimes the things that are hardest to let go are the places God needs to break through most.

KEY VERSES:
"But thanks be to God that, though you used to be slaves to sin, you have come to obey from your heart the pattern of teaching that has now claimed your allegiance. You have been set free from sin and have become slaves to righteousness."
Romans 6:17-18

REFLECTION QUESTIONS:
+ Brianna got so caught up in chasing after an image of individuality and independence that in the end left her feeling isolated and alone. Can you think of a time in your life where you fought for a certain identity? How does fighting for an identity outside of Christ leave us feeling?

DAY 3

Once Brianna got plugged into community, she realized that it was a piece of her obedience in Christ. It is easy to forget that the way God wants us to live is really meant to bring us life. Obedience may, at first, feel like letting go of your own freedoms for a higher purpose, more of a sacrifice. But what if we looked at obedience as a key to unlock God's best for our lives? A parent who truly loves you makes rules and guidelines because they know what's best for you. God knew it was best for Brianna to immerse herself in community. Our heart changes when we understand the intentions behind the "rules." When our mom tells us not to date a boy, we can look back and thank her because she saved our heart from hurt. When our parents insist we come back home by 11, as adults, we can understand it was to keep us out of temptation. Being obedient is taking a step in maturity and choosing to live a life that reflects the God we love and serve. When we choose obedience we have nothing to be ashamed of and in turn experience pure joy. Like Jesus' obedience at the cross, "for the joy set before him, he endured the cross." Our obedience, no matter how uncomfortable or painful it may feel at the time, leads to ultimate joy because we are pursuing the will of the Father.

KEY VERSES:
"And surely I am with you always, to the very end of the age."
Matthew 28:20b

REFLECTION QUESTIONS:
+ For most of us growing up, obedience had a negative connotation when it came to curfews and report cards, but how does obedience to God look different? How can you see obedience as a joyful effort in drawing closer to Him, rather than a set of rules to follow? Do you have faith that the Lord has a greater plan in mind when you choose to be obedient?

DAY 4

Righteousness is a word thrown around a lot, but what does it mean? It means to be in right standing with God. All over the Bible God calls us righteous. We are in right standing with Him. No matter what we did yesterday or do tomorrow we are made right with Him. Not because of how many hours we spent with God that week or Bible verses we Instagrammed—we are secure and made right with Him. It is so hard to understand a love like His, one we do not have to earn. Even our best friend's have earned their way to the top—great memories, roommates, family vacations, the time spent getting to know each other has grown into a relationship with a mutual understanding of where you stand. You don't need to ask your best friend if she'll help you pick out a dress, just tell her what time you are picking her up. It's hard to imagine a God we've never seen, had sleepovers with, or had classes with could care so intimately about our hearts. But He does. Who you believe God to be is the most important perspective of your life. I challenge you to set aside a time where it's just you and God everyday for the rest of the school year. Meet with Him on your back porch, at your favorite coffee shop, for the sunrise at your favorite beach. Every day write down a different character trait or personality trait of the God you are getting to know. Ask Him to reveal to you the places He wants you to let go and grow into His likeness in obedience to who He is.

KEY VERSES:
"My heart says of you, "Seek his face!" Your face, Lord, I will seek."
Psalm 27:8

REFLECTION QUESTIONS:
+ How can you begin to let go of your self-focused mindset and instead, walk in obedience for the Lord? Have you been missing something that the Lord has been telling you because you've been so concerned with yourself? What might obedience for the Lord look like in your life right now?

SHELBY

SAM HOUSTON STATE UNIVERSITY
INTERNATIONAL BUSINESS
SENIOR

Overcoming Jealousy

LEARNING TO SEE THE CHRIST-LIKE QUALITIES IN YOUR FRIENDS

I've heard it said, "You don't go to college to meet your husband. You go to college to meet your bridesmaids." Coming to college that's exactly what I was excited about. My whole life I've longed for a "best friend" or a close set of friends who would understand me and love me well. That's why I was so excited when in the first few weeks of school I was introduced to some of the coolest people I had ever met. They were girls with genuine smiles, avid Chaco-wearers, and they spoke about Jesus as if He was in the room with them. I knew that this would be the place where I would finally meet my life-long friends that I had always desired.

"How good and pleasant it is when God's people live together in unity!"
Psalm 133:1

A few weeks into my freshman year, I joined a small group of girls to study the Word with weekly. I was encouraged and loved in ways that I never knew were possible. All the girls in our group became super close within a short amount of time. We started to do everything together; our joy was unrelenting and our laughter was ab-creating; friendship had never been so sweet. We spent more time hammocking on campus than in our classes. Taryn, my small group leader, held craft nights and game nights, inviting any and everyone. My friend Kerrie and I's love for adrenaline would get the best of us, and we would end up long boarding for hours upon hours. Some of my sweetest memories consisted of late night Whataburger runs with Taryn or Eleanor that would end with us chatting in the car until the wee hours of the morning. These were the college adventures I had always longed for.

The closer I grew to a friend, the closer I began to draw to Christ because I could see a new characteristic of the Lord. One showed Grace. Another was Precious, another Nurturing, another Humorous, and so on. My desire for friendship and fellowship grew at an exponential rate, so it should come as no surprise that friend dates became more common than dates with my homework.

"As iron sharpens iron, so one person sharpens another."
Proverbs 27:17

Day after day our community began to grow, the Lord's Kingdom was expanding, and when I spent time with these friends that I now called my sisters, my heart was so full. After a while that fullness came with a twinge of bitterness. At first I didn't notice the bitterness in my own heart because it was a feeling that I would push away. I noticed that I had begun to hide feelings from friends, and after more time, I even began to hide my face by not spending time with my friends. I did not want to bring attention to my feelings, but admittedly, I wanted my friends to bring their attention to me, to seek me out. Our group had grown so large that I felt as if I was lost in the crowd, the best friends that I had developed deep and meaningful friendships with over the previous months were now friends with everyone else. That was a hard thing to swallow.

Remember how I told you I had longed for best friends all my life, what I didn't realize was that with the world's view of "best friends" often comes a lot of jealousy. Jealousy is a tool Satan uses to destroy and divide relationships; we become destructive instead of constructive.

"The thief comes only to steal and kill and destroy; I have come that they may have life, and have it to the full."
John 10:10

The thief had come to kill my desires, steal my joy, and destroy my friendships. My goal went from uplifting my sisters in Jesus' name, to becoming obsessed with having more and more friends. I was full of selfishness and pride. I had lost all vulnerability and depth with my friends because I was hidden behind embarrassment and bitterness that was based off of pure selfish reasoning.

Like the older son in the parable of the lost son (John 15:11-32), when someone was welcomed into the family I became angry because attention and celebration was elsewhere. This anger caused a wall to rise up around my heart and gave me an attitude where I resisted the responsibility to pray for, laugh, and celebrate with my sisters. I didn't want to see their friendship develop because I thought it meant I would be left behind. I felt as if what I had to offer to the group was no longer good and worthy.

Looking back, this was the point where I had pulled so far from the group, that I had begun to destroy the friendships that God head built for me in the months prior. I came to see that if we are not building His Kingdom, we are destroying it. The biggest lie that I had begun to believe was that I was the only one with jealous feelings. I kept to thinking to myself, "Why was everyone so perfect in creating and maintaining a friendship?" I felt as if I couldn't come before the Lord with my feelings of jealousy because of pride and shame and fear of disappointing God.

"He is jealous for me.
Love's like a hurricane, I am a tree.
Bending beneath the waves of His wind and mercy.
When all of a sudden, I am unaware of
these afflictions eclipsed by Glory.
And I realize just how beautiful You are and
How great Your affections are for me.
Oh, how He loves me. Oh, how He loves me. How he loves me, so."

These words were blaring in my headphones while riding in the back of a truck one day, and I came to the realization that the Lord was jealous for me. "Wait, for me? He, the Creator of the Universe and King of all the World, was jealous for my attention and my affection. But why?"

I had given all I had and all I was to so many friends and hobbies for so long only to leave God on the back burner. The more I thought about it the more it pierced at my heart and gave me a deeper desire to know my Father's heart. He experienced jealousy, and I was left speechless. If no one could ever relate to me, it didn't matter because my Heavenly Father could on some level.

I began to understand how God's jealousy stems from a place of deep love. God ultimately took the biggest risk in allowing us to be beings that have free will to come and go as we please, taking and using his love and grace when we need it. Even though He is all powerful, He chose not to control us and force us into relations with Him but rather stands with open arms ready for us to run to Him at any moment. He is jealous for us to return to Him, to choose Him over the things of this world. God's jealousy is drenched in His perfect love.

"For the LORD your God is a consuming fire, a jealous God."
Deuteronomy 4:24

My jealousy, on the other hand, was stemming from a place of fear. Fear of rejection, being left out, and being misunderstood. I needed to allow the Lord to break down my walls of bitterness and break my chains of "me-centered-jealousy."

First, I knew that needed to be vulnerable with my friends because of How Jesus had revealed his vulnerability to me. I got on my knees and asked the Lord to take myself off the throne of my heart, Jesus off the cross of my heart and replace the throne with Himself and the cross with me.

Friendship is a gift meant to reflect the heart of our Father in Heaven, so "Lord, help me die to myself daily and forgive me for placing myself at the center of attention. Show me how to love your children."

I got up to face the challenge I had been keeping a secret for months. Little did I know that as soon as I was vulnerable with my friends about the jealousy that had been eating away at me, they too would admit their struggles with jealousy.

Through this experience, I learned that a friendship could only be as deep as the depth of myself that I'm willing to share. We are who we are because of the experiences we have experienced and the events that we have walked through, but people won't know these things if we aren't willing to share them. God calls us to be vulnerable with the people around us about our insecurities, our fears, and the sometimes crazy things going on in our minds. You can't always expect your friends to approach you about how you're doing. But sometimes when you're brave enough to be the first to admit your mess you open the door for others to be vulnerable with you in return. True friendship is honest, real, and welcomes vulnerability.

Today, instead of being jealous of my friends and trying to break their friendships apart, I can thank the Lord for their friendship, their friendship with each other, and that the Lord's character is revealed in each of them. If each one of us is a part of the Lord that has never been seen before and will never be seen again, then why would I want to miss what the Lord is trying to show all of us.

"But because of his great love for us, God, who is rich in mercy, made us alive with Christ even when we were dead in transgressions—it is by grace you have been saved."
Ephesians 2:4-5

If you are anything like me, the first response to jealousy is not prayer and praise, but I promise the first prayer you pray over your jealousy toward a friend will create a new heart in you. You will begin to see them with the Father's eyes, and you rejoice with the Father over His beautiful daughter and how her life reflects His love.

Know you are not alone, so do not isolate yourself from the fellowship the Lord has given you. You are important to others. You carry a part of the Lord that everyone needs. We might not be able to be best friends with everyone, but we can all be best friends with the Author of friendship and fellowship. He knows your every need and desires your attention with all His heart.

KEY VERSES:
Psalm 133:1
Proverbs 27:17
John 10:10
Deuteronomy 4:24
Ephesians 2:4-5
John 15:11-32

DISCUSSION QUESTIONS:
+ Coming to college, what were your expectations of friendships? What did you picture your friendships looking like? Who did you picture yourself being friends with?
+ Shelby found the friends she had always wanted, but after some time, jealousy began to sneak into those relationships. Have you experienced jealousy in your friendships? Where did that jealousy stem from? Was it a fear of being left out, fear of rejection, being misunderstood, etc.?
+ What walls is jealously creating in your friendships? Instead of letting them affect your relationships, how can you begin to be more expressive about what you are dealing with? What might you need to share with your friends today to break down those walls?
+When we begin to look for the Lord's character in our friends, we are less tempted to let jealousy stand in the way. Think about each one of your friends and what specific characteristics of the Lord they show you. How might focusing on these qualities change the way you view them?
+ How often do you pray for your friendships? How often do you pray against jealousy? Is there a specific situation that you need to be honest with the Lord about? How might talking to Him change your perspective on this?

DEVOTIONALS

CONTRIBUTOR: *Tiffany Rybka*

DAY 1

Expectations can be a dangerous thing because, more often than not, expectations simply aren't met. Whether the expectation that we have is for ourselves, a relationship, an experience, or something else, reality often falls short of our expectations and therefore leaves us feeling disappointed. Even if the reality of the situation is a good thing, still we might find ourselves blinded to that because it isn't the great thing that we were hoping for and dreaming of. So not only do expectations set us up for disappointment, but also, they can cause us to miss the good things that God places in our paths instead.

Expectations can also be dangerous because, even if things work out the way we want them to, we will never be fully satisfied by the fulfillment of worldly expectations. Like in Shelby's story, there may be times in our lives where we get the relationships and adventures that we always desired, but still, there will always be something that "could be better." Expectations set us up for disappointment, but they also set us up for jealousy. Whatever it is in our lives that we think "could be better," we will tend to compare with those who we think have it better. This jealousy will not only eat us up inside, but it will also cause conflict between ourselves and those we compare ourselves to.

Rather than challenging yourself to get rid of your expectations instead evaluate how you handle your expectations. Are they causing you to be blinded to the other good things in your life? Are they causing you to let conflict get in the way of your relationships? If so, push those expectations to the side, at least for a while, and be intentional in enjoying the gifts that God has placed in your life!

KEY VERSES:
"The thief comes only to steal and kill and destroy; I have come that they may have life, and have it to the full."
John 10:10

REFLECTION QUESTIONS:

+ Coming to college, what were your expectations of friendships? What did you picture your friendships looking like? Who did you picture yourself being friends with?

+ Shelby found the friends she had always wanted, but after some time jealousy began to sneak into those relationships. Have you experienced jealousy in your friendships? Where did that jealousy stem from? Was it a fear of being left out, fear of rejection, being misunderstood, etc.?

DAY 2

C.S. Lewis says this: *"To love at all is to be vulnerable. Love anything and your heart will be wrung and possibly broken. If you want to make sure of keeping it intact you must give it to no one, not even an animal. Wrap it carefully round with hobbies and little luxuries; avoid all entanglements. Lock it up safe in the casket or coffin of your selfishness. But in that casket, safe, dark, motionless, airless, it will change. It will not be broken; it will become unbreakable, impenetrable, irredeemable. To love is to be vulnerable."*

In Shelby's story, her decision to be vulnerable about her insecurities was in many ways the turning point of her story. Not only did her vulnerability break the bondage of jealousy that she had been stuck in for months, but it set a tone of vulnerability among her friends too! Oftentimes, we steer clear of vulnerability due to fear—fear of rejection, of being misunderstood, of what our friends might think, and so on. But, in reality, vulnerability shows strengths and leadership more than it shows weakness. To be vulnerable is to put ourselves out there, not as who we want people to see us but as who we really are. And that takes guts. Vulnerability is scary and it takes a lot of bravery, but it is something that real relationships can't survive without. Are you willing to be a leader in vulnerability?

KEY VERSES:
"How good and pleasant it is when God's people live together in unity!"
Psalm 133:1

"There is no fear in love. But perfect love drives out fear, because fear has to do with punishment. The one who fears is not made perfect in love."
1 John 4:18

REFLECTION QUESTION:
+ What walls is jealously creating in your friendships? Instead of letting them affect your relationships, how can you begin to be more expressive about what you are dealing with? What might you need to share with your friends today to break down those walls?

Shelby talks in her story about how the closer she drew to her new friends, the closer she drew to God, because she saw a new characteristic of God in each of her friends. She writes: *"If each one of us is a part of the Lord that has never been seen before and will never be seen again, then why would I want to miss what the Lord is trying to show all of us?"*

How incredible is that? This is what Christian friendship, Christian sisterhood, is intended to look like, reflecting God's love to each other and, as a result, reflecting God's love to the world. This is incredible enough, but even more incredible than that, is the fact that we all reflect God's love and character in different ways. And this is not just a coincidence, but rather, this is part of His unique design for each of us! Isn't it wonderful to be one of God's daughters?

Just like we can be leaders in vulnerability when it comes to the negative feelings in our hearts and thoughts in our mind, we can also be leaders in vulnerability when it comes to the positive things (for example, sharing with each of your friends how you see them reflecting God's love and character to you and to the world around them!). Maybe even consider getting your group of friends together and taking turns sharing these characteristics with each other publicly. I can guarantee you that this would result in a special memory for all of you, and a greater love and appreciation for each other's unique designs!

KEY VERSES:
"As iron sharpens iron, so one person sharpens another."
Proverbs 27:17

REFLECTION QUESTIONS:
+ When we begin to look for the Lord's character in our friends, we are less tempted to let jealousy stand in the way. Think about each one of your friends and what specific characteristics of the Lord they show you. How might focusing on these qualities change the way you view them?

Just like all good things, real Christian friendships take time and effort. Why? Because real Christian friendships, or real Christian relationships of any kind, are an excellent and praiseworthy thing; therefore they are susceptible to Satan's attacks! Satan wants us to be jealous. He *wants* us to be insecure. He *wants* us to feel alone, and he *wants* these things to drive us further and further away from each other rather than closer and closer together. There is power in numbers in worldly battles, and the same is true for spiritual battles. The more that we love each other, and the more that we are honest and vulnerable with each other, the more strength we will have to fight against spiritual attacks. This is another one of God's incredible intentions for Christian relationships.

So how can we protect our Christian friendships? Going back to battle terms, in Ephesians 6 the Apostle Paul lists off the armor of God, which can help us stand against the Father of Lies' evil schemes. He finishes this list off, though, with these words: *"And pray in the Spirit on all occasions with all kinds of prayers and requests. With this in mind, be alert and always keep on praying for all the Lord's people"* (Ephesians 6:18). The best thing that we can do to protect our Christian friendships is to *pray*; to pray against jealousy, insecurities, loneliness, comparison, disunity. By praying constantly, we keep Jesus at the forefront of our minds and therefore at the forefront of our relationships with other people. We must keep an eternal perspective in all things!

KEY VERSES:
"But because of his great love for us, God, who is rich in mercy, made us alive with Christ even when we were dead in transgressions – it is by grace you have been saved."
Ephesians 2:4-5

REFLECTION QUESTIONS:
+ How often do you pray for your friendships? How often do you pray against jealousy? Is there a specific situation that you need to be honest with the Lord about? How might talking to Him change your perspective on this?

An Authentic Christian

LEARNING TO FOLLOW CHRIST OVER CHRISTIAN CULTURE

"Do not conform to the pattern of this world, but be transformed by the renewing of your mind. Then you will be able to test and approve what God's will is—his good, pleasing and perfect will."
Romans 12:2

Have you ever dreamed of the person that you wanted to be one day? When you're little, you imagine the occupation that you want do: an astronaut, a teacher, a doctor, or in my case, a dolphin trainer. We dream ourselves into these roles by flying to the moon, listening to the heartbeat of our pet, and by playing these roles just for a little bit, we began to truly believe that this is who we are.

As I've gotten older, I still find myself dreaming of who I could be one day. When I became a Christian, I began to think about the kind of character that I wanted to have in the future. I wanted to grow into a "great" Christian. As I was leaving for college, I had the expectation that my potential experiences and relationships in Stillwater at Oklahoma State University would give me the growth that I needed to finally embody who I thought I should be in Christ.

Within my first weeks in Stillwater, I was lucky enough to be surrounded by a wonderful group of women—some my age and some older. Naturally and thankfully, the older girls started taking us to Bible studies, clubs, and churches in town. As the semester progressed, I was only exposed to a relatively small group of Christians on campus, so I came to a conclusion that this was the only way to live out my faith well in college. I placed these women, who were only a year or two older than me, on a pedestal and measured myself to them and their lifestyles. I hung tightly to the hope that if I followed their footsteps, then when I was their age I would be the same kind of Christian that everyone looked up to. I studied and followed their footsteps carefully, believing that these things would allow me to grow in intimacy with Christ, but at the same time, I was neglecting my own time with Christ. Instead of using the Bible as truth, I allowed these girls and my perception of them become what directed my life and my judgment in making decisions.

For my freshman and sophomore year of college, I did exactly that. At first, I loved all the new opportunities and options that I had. I jumped in to anything that I could, and everything around me told me that being busy was good; being busy would get you a jumpstart in your career; being involved in at least three ministries, leading a Bible study for middle school girls, and committing to clubs on campus was a normal thing for college students. And somehow, I was also supposed to have time for friendships and time with God and time to breathe too. I kept on pressing on though because I thought this was what it looked like to be a Christian at OSU. This was the example that was left before me, so I followed it. And at best, I felt like I was drowning. I put all of my effort into what I thought would develop me into a "great" Christian—I followed girls into their ministries, answered with the right answers whenever they asked, and spread myself thin over classes, friendships, and time.

"Yet when I surveyed all that my hands had done and what I had toiled to achieve, everything was meaningless, a chasing after the wind; nothing was gained under the sun."
Ecclesiastes 2:11

I was chasing this illusion that I could be a "great" Christian by living like this, but in reality, I was exhausted trying to make myself into something I was not. I did not spend time with the Lord unless it was required of me to either lead a Bible study or to meet with a mentor. I went to the same church as everyone else, even if I didn't relate to the teaching because it was the easy thing to do. During this time, I was aware that something wasn't right. I didn't want to spend any time with the Lord. I didn't have time for relationships. I was constantly exhausted of everything, but I never dwelled upon why this wasn't right long enough to realize that I was following the culture of a Christian rather than Christ.

I finally came to a day at the end of February of my sophomore year; nothing was special about that day except for I chose to be still for more than ten minutes. I thought about who I wanted to be, thought I was, and the reality of who I had become in the past year and a half. I felt like I was doing everything right and that all of this would be pleasing to God. I had been executing to my best ability what I thought I should be doing as a Christian, and yet I still felt deeply empty. I came across this passage:

"As Jesus and his disciples were on their way, he came to a village where a woman named Martha opened her home to him. She had a sister called Mary,who sat at the Lord's feet listening to what he said. But Martha was distracted by all the preparations that had to be made. She came to him and asked, "Lord, don't you care that my sister has left me to do the work by myself? Tell her to help me!"

"Martha, Martha," the Lord answered, "you are worried and upset about many things, but few things are needed—or indeed only one. Mary has chosen what is better, and it will not be taken away from her."
Luke 10:38-42

No matter how many great and godly organizations I was in or how I believed that those alone would draw me nearer to God, I was a slave to this world's idea of who a Christian should be. Like Martha, I worked and served as much as I could, thinking that by doing this I would please the Lord; instead, we both missed the heart of Jesus in this moment. When I thought that I had to do these certain things to prove that I was a Christian, to live up to expectations, or to follow a Christian culture, I missed out on the incredible intimacy that Jesus offers because I was "worried and bothered about so many things." And what was the truth that Jesus reminds Martha? "Only one thing is necessary," and we, like Mary, can choose to abandon what culture tells us to do and instead live in the presence of Jesus and His freedom!

This acknowledgment that I wasn't living for the Lord but rather to please others and to assimilate into a crooked culture was the most honest I had been with myself. By realizing that I was chasing after a culture instead of God, the Lord revealed to me how I limited His power in my life. Because I believed for so long that Christianity could only look one way and that was the example of the girls before me, I bypassed opportunities and instead pursued an image within one specific Christian context—only to gain me a uniformed identity with the people around me. I secluded myself to a certain group of Christians on campus; I tried to morph my gifts and talents into something that they weren't because I was trying to rigidly follow the example set before me by other girls. I no longer looked to Christ for truth but only looked to see how I could serve Christ by means of culture. I missed opportunities to what God could have done through me if I were honest with myself.

Over time, I unknowingly traded my freedom in Christ for the binds of culture and the idea of what I thought a "great" Christian should look like. I traded in who the Lord made me to be for expectations and ideas of what I thought Christianity looked like at Oklahoma State—which was getting recruited by a specific sorority, wearing certain brands, hanging out at the local coffee shop, going to worship every Tuesday night, serving particular ministries, and not going to parties. I told myself that I could be a "great" Christian if I acted within this structure, but I limited God by secluding Him to a specific culture and believed in a lie by placing Him there.

"He exerted when he raised Christ from the dead and seated him at his right hand in the heavenly realms, far above all rule and authority, power and dominion, and every name that is invoked, not only in the present age but also in the one to come."
Ephesians 1:20b-21

I've come to realize that God is above anything that we can create here, even the Christian culture that we can find ourselves in. I left myself completely vulnerable for culture and expectations to mold my perception of a Christian life.
I spent my time becoming someone I thought I should be instead of embracing my own gifts and talents; I shifted my foundation of Christ to a foundation of deception and accepted lies that having Christ alone wasn't good enough but that I needed to become all these things in order to have a "great" relationship with Christ. This change in my mind was so subtle. It took me almost two years to realize how far I had removed myself from God's heart. God created the world and everything within it. He is above anything that we try to fit Him, and if/when I do try to find Him in a culture, I'm only accepting a lie and limiting what God can do in my life.

After learning this truth, I evaluated everything I was doing and why I was doing it—did I enjoy it or was I doing a certain ministry because that is what everyone else was doing? Since then, I've stepped down from certain roles, and it's been really hard, but I know that someone else more passionate than me is replacing me in that ministry or club. I am learning to carve out time to sit, be still, and be reminded of who God is without the help of my peers or from culture. I have stopped doing things that I had expected other people to see and think, "Wow, she's a 'great' Christian" (even writing that makes me cringe), but I know that no matter what I do if it's not for the Lord, it's for nothing. I even got a little extreme once, thinking that I only wanted to do something that would be just for me and God, and I signed up for a five hundred mile bike tour that would benefit a nonprofit; hardly anyone understood why I was doing it, but I chose to take that risk, and the Lord revealed His faithfulness and His overwhelming love to me and so many others in a new way. By no longer pretending to have this relationship with God, it's crazy; I actually get to enjoy a relationship with the living God instead of feeling burdened by what I'm supposed to do. Living like Martha exhausted me, so now I want to live like Mary, choosing to be at Jesus' feet and ready to obey, serve, and love Him.

"So that Christ may dwell in your hearts through faith. And I pray that you, being rooted and established in love, may have power, together with all the Lord's holy people, to grasp how wide and long and high and deep is the love of Christ, and to know this love that surpasses knowledge— that you may be filled to the measure of all the fullness of God."
Ephesians 3:17-19

I think it's hard to catch yourself changing in order to fit in. For some, it may be more obvious by showing it on the exterior. For me, it was a desire of mine to be in a spiritual place that I wasn't at that time, and so I did everything I could to try to be this certain type of Christian woman that others could look up to. This pattern became so habitual that it took me too long to notice it. I encourage each of you to check on what foundation you are building your life upon—Christ's or culture's. By trading in the deception of the Christian culture for Christ, I have found once again the freedom of who Jesus is, and I am able to have authenticity in my relationships and in sharing the Gospel.

Time and time again, God reminds me of this beautiful truth: we are only the earthly vessels for our infinite God, who cannot be bound to time, culture, or this world, and He continually lavishes us in His forgiveness, love, and grace.

KEY VERSES:

Romans 12:2
Ecclesiastes 2:11
Luke 10:38-42
Ephesians 1:20b-21
Ephesians 3:17-19

DISCUSSION QUESTIONS:

+ Who or what do you think of when you hear the term "great" Christian? In your mind, what characteristics or qualities "qualifies" a "great" Christian?

+ During your time in college, have you found yourself following a path other people have set? When making decisions do you think of what "they" would do or what Christ calls you to do? Think of decisions from your past that have been influenced by people rather than God.

+ Reggie chased the illusion that she could be a "great" Christian by doing certain things, but in reality, she was exhausted trying to make herself into something she wasn't. What things are you doing in your life right now that are leaving you exhausted? Are you doing these things because the Lord is calling you to them or because you see everybody else doing them?

+ How are you limiting what God can do in your life by secluding Him to a specific culture? How would your life look different if you stopped following Christian culture?

+ When we no longer live within the confinements of Christian culture, we get to enjoy a real relationship with the Living God rather than feeling burdened by what we're supposed to do. What burdens do you need to let go of today to actually enjoy your relationship with Jesus? How can you spend the rest of your time in college embracing the unique path that God has designed for you?

DEVOTIONALS

CONTRIBUTOR: *Makayla White*

DAY 1

There is a difference between challenging yourself to grow in Christ and forcing yourself to be as much like your Christian mentor as possible. Instead of inviting our Maker into our life decisions, we look to the "great" Christians that we have, like Reggie, placed on the pedestal of our lives. Let's call this what it is: an idol. The second we place who "they" are above who we are in Christ, we spiral into a place that God never intended for us. It is easy to consider others and how they got to where we see them today instead of looking to the beauty filled path God has for us. There is a unique definition of you that Christ has destined that can be suffocated by chasing after your idea of a "great" Christian. Taking the others-focused strong hold off of our lives can allow us to breathe in, deeply and freely, the life-giving plan of the Father.

KEY VERSES:
"Do not conform to the pattern of this world, but be transformed by the renewing of your mind. Then you will be able to test and approve what God's will is—his good, pleasing and perfect will."
Romans 12:2

REFLECTION QUESTIONS:
+ Who or what do you think of when you hear the term "great" Christian? In your mind, what characteristics or qualities "qualifies" a "great" Christian?
+ During your time in college have you found yourself following a path other people have set? When making decisions do you think of what "they" would do or what Christ calls you to do? Think of decisions from your past that have been influenced by people rather than God.

Exhausted. Tired. Drained. These are places that the Lord never wants us to be. He came so "that they may have life, and have it to the full" (John 10:10). This verse clearly does not say, "They may work their whole lives trying to prove themselves." Reggie compares herself to the character of Martha, who was distracted by meaningless toil rather than sitting at the feet of Jesus. At its root, distracted means "to drag around." Sometimes that is exactly what exhaustion feels like, being drug around. In order to be drug around, you have to have yourself attached to something. If you are finding yourself at the end of your rope, maybe it is time to take a step back and see what you have it tied to.

KEY VERSES:
"Yet when I surveyed all that my hands had done and what I had toiled to achieve, everything was meaningless, a chasing after the wind; nothing was gained under the sun."
Ecclesiastes 2:11

REFLECTION QUESTIONS:
+ Reggie chased the illusion that she could be a "great" Christian by doing certain things, but in reality, she was exhausted trying to make herself into something she wasn't. What things are you doing in your life right now that are leaving you exhausted? Are you doing these things because the Lord is calling you to them or because you see everybody else doing them?

The Christian culture box that we place God into is usually based on our knowledge of who God is to other people and what we are "supposed" to do to become the Christians they are. But all of this places our human expectations on who God is and what our relationship with Him can be. God doesn't want to simply fit into the box that our capabilities of understanding construct. He wants to expand beyond our comprehension and show us wonders that we could not even imagine. He wants to fill us with a fullness that no aspect of Christian culture can anticipate. "...to know this love that surpasses knowledge—that you may be filled to the measure of all the fullness of God" (Ephesians 3:19). Imagine the limitless life of fullness, love, and passion that God could overwhelm you with if you stopped trying to fill your life with "to-do's" and "to-be's," which He never intended for you to do or to be.

KEY VERSES:
"So that Christ may dwell in your hearts through faith. And I pray that you, being rooted and established in love, may have power, together with all the Lord's holy people, to grasp how wide and long and high and deep is the love of Christ, and to know this love that surpasses knowledge— that you may be filled to the measure of all the fullness of God."
Ephesians 3:17-19

REFLECTION QUESTIONS:
+ How are you limiting what God can do in your life by secluding Him to a specific culture? How would your life look different if you stopped following Christian culture?

DAY 4

You were custom made for a divine purpose, and it was not to be burdened by living up to the expectations of others, even those in your most trusted circle of Christian community. The path you walk together can be headed in the same direction without looking the exact same. Relationships filled with love, understanding, and wisdom can revolve around Christ without placing the burden of expectations on your shoulders. What is your picture of the perfect, Christian college woman? Have you placed these expectations on yourself? Is the load getting heavy? That's because it was never meant for you. Take it off. Let it go. Sit at the feet of the Father, looking only at Him, ask what He has for you today.

KEY VERSES:
"He exerted when he raised Christ from the dead and seated him at his right hand in the heavenly realms, far above all rule and authority, power and dominion, and every name that is invoked, not only in the present age but also in the one to come."
Ephesians 1:20-21

REFLECTION QUESTIONS:
+ When we no longer live within the confinements of Christian culture, we get to enjoy a real relationship with the Living God rather than feeling burdened by what we're supposed to do. What burdens do you need to let go of today to actually enjoy your relationship with Jesus? How can you spend the rest of your time in college embracing the unique path that God has designed for you?

MADI

CAL POLY SLO
COMMUNICATIONS STUDIES
FRESHMAN

Overwhelming Grace

FIGHTING SHAME AND SIN

I'm the type of girl who can't get enough of adventure. I'm talking, spontaneous camping trips up the coast. I'm talking "borrowing" a campus golf cart for the evening to the top of the campus valley for some sunset serenity. I crave fun, and I crave doing it alongside people who know and love me. When I'm side by side with those people, in the midst of nature, with an adventure ahead, I truly feel fearless. I have nothing to hide, I feel authentically free.

To be honest, real life isn't always like that for me. I came into college with the mindset of going on a lot of adventures but also with the mindset of following God. I was ready for a new pace, to go on adventures with friends while also refreshing my spirituality. I grew up going to private school my whole life, surrounded by the same 300 people. A big public school seemed like the perfect next adventure to embark on. But I came in knowing it was gonna be an uphill battle and a lonely one at that. I am a recovering perfectionist, striving to strive less; working towards not working for my worth. I was unsure of how God felt about me and unsure about the whole Christian faith. Either way, I was alone.

I remember walking to CRU— a college campus ministry— the first week of college with my roommate shaking in shame. I had a senior year of mistakes and sexual sin that drove a wedge between God and I that made even the entrance of a church seem like an execution chamber.

"She will chase after her lovers but not catch them; she will look for them but not find them. Then she will say, 'I will go back to my husband as at first, for then I was better off than now.' She has not acknowledged that I was the one who gave her the grain, the new wine and oil, who lavished on her the silver and gold— which they used for Baal."
Hosea 2:7-8

I was constantly surrounded by good hearted, inspiring people, but I constantly felt alone and misunderstood. I repressed these feelings as much as possible, until I crossed paths with her. Through a friend of an acquaintance, I met Rebecca. She invited me to her sorority's bible study that week. Again, I was nervous, I was afraid I would be found out, that I would be seen. Somehow I ended up in that cozy room sitting next to ten women I had never met. Right off the bat, Rebecca played a video about vulnerability and the importance of being seen and known.

My stomach dropped. *No, not this. Please. No.*

She continued by breaking us up in groups and encouraged us to share what we have been struggling with. With my heart beating, I knew I needed to share what had been going on. But I couldn't. I couldn't risk being seen like this. It was too risky.

While I blamed it on the circumstances, the timing, the environment, my shame was winning. *What would happen if they really saw me in all of my sin? Will they like me after that? Will God love me after that?*

The bible study ended (thankfully), and I had slid in by unseen. Or so I thought.

After the study, Rebecca asked if she could take me home. I got in the car, and she immediately started talking, "I am so excited to get to know you, and I am excited to share my story with you. My whole life, I had struggled with masturbation and sexual sin."

I stopped breathing.

My whole life I have never had anyone talk so openly about something I have struggled with. I have never had someone acknowledge it.

I sat there nodding my head as my eyes welded up. I whispered, *me too.*

Those two words were the beginning of a whole new chapter of my life. I started from the beginning, sharing the shame that I felt, the isolation. I didn't think I was worthy of any love because of my sin, because I was so human. I believed the lie that I will never be more than what I've done. The power of having another person share in my shame, to come down in the darkness with me and show me that I am not alone brought a freedom to my life I never thought was possible.

In that moment of honesty, where I told another human about my shame, I was set free because I was loved and accepted in all my imperfections.

It was when I exposed my true self that I could experience what Jesus meant when he talked about freedom. My whole freshman year I have been wrestling with the thought that Jesus actually loves me despite what I do, that there is always grace and love for me, that nothing I can do can separate me from him.

Man, this truly scares me.

How am I supposed to believe I am a worthy of God's love if I am not doing anything explicit that could make him love me? All my life I thought I had to earn this, when in reality grace was it. I called my counselor to discuss all my thoughts. And I will never forget what they said. "The only thing holding you back is that you don't believe that you are worthy. You are questioning this grace. You are trying to put it in a formula so it makes sense. You will never understand grace. But you can't experience freedom if you never accept God's love."

A lot of what I have experienced reminds me of the story of Hosea. God sends a faithful man to pursue a prostitute. She runs away after she marries Hosea to a different man and sells herself to him. But Hosea doesn't give up. He runs after her, buys her back, and takes her back. Despite everything.

"Therefore I am now going to allure her; I will lead her into the wilderness and speak tenderly to her. There I will give her back her vineyards, and will make the Valley of Achor a door of hope. There she will respond as in the days of her youth, as in the day she came up out of Egypt."
Hosea 2:14-15

We are not loved because of anything we do. Nothing. We are accepted by God and all He asks us to do is come as we are.

A few months after this conversation happened, I sort of forgot that I would need grace again in my life. I kind of assumed it was a one and done deal. That I was forgiven and I would never mess up again.

One Saturday night, I was tempted again. The next morning I woke up covered in shame again. I scolded myself. Again? Really Madi? You know better.

Sitting in church that morning was probably the worst part. I was there, in all my shame, looking at everyone singing and knowing I wasn't worthy of being there. Everyone else was a faithful Christian and I was a sinful, selfish person. But as I sat there, something fought back.

No, Madi. You are enough. You are exactly who you are supposed to be right now. I am teaching you grace.

In the first two worship songs, I couldn't even mutter a word. And then with a helpless voice, I sung my first broken hallelujah. I didn't sing with the thought that I was worthy. I sung a cry of help, of desire for change. I slowly lifted my hands in front of my chest and surrendered my sin.

I not only shared in a me too moment with Rebecca, I shared a me too moment with Jesus. He was there in it with me.

"When hard pressed, I cried to the LORD; he brought me into a spacious place."
Psalm 118:5

I did not need to clean myself up before coming to Him. I didn't need to try and fix my problems and sin and do everything on my own. Jesus was there in it, and He is always there to give grace, to offer that hope. He died so I could come to Him and be forgiven.

This concept is literally so simple, but the most difficult thing to actually practice. It is why Jesus died; it is why I have freedom. We can come in our most shameful times and say, Help. I need you.

That is all God asks of us. To come to Him and He will transform our lives and give us freedom.

"Come to me, all you who are weary and burdened, and I will give you rest."
Matthew 11:28

I had to come to terms with the different between guilt and shame. When I came to God that day in church, I was full of shame. But shame is not from God. Shame calls us into isolation and holds us down in the darkness of our sin. Guilt pushes us towards confession and says, "This is not what I have for you."

I am slowly feeling less and less shame when I make mistakes, rather my heart is slowly wanting to make the right decision because of how precious and beautiful grace is. God pursues us like Hosea. Taking our mistakes and making them part of His story to show grace and acceptance. He wants to demonstrate His love for us like a lover, instead of having us work for our worth and His love like servants.

"I will betroth you to me forever;   I will betroth you in righteousness and justice, in love and compassion."
Hosea 2:19

It is so beautiful that God refers to Israel as his wife. The whole concept is so crazy to understand, but the only thing we can do is accept it. He will do the work. He will change our hearts. We just have to come as we are, surrender, and let Him clean us up.

It's not like I haven't sinned since I experienced God's grace. It's not like I don't struggle with temptation anymore. But now I realize that God wants to be with me in the midst of my sin, temptation, and when I am tempted, to call to Him and ask for help. To say, God, please be with me in this and change my heart.

There is so much power in letting Him come into our sin and let Him heal us from our shame.

The amazing thing about grace is that is lightens our hearts from the burden of shame. It also allows us to relate to other people and be a Rebecca. There is freedom in, Me too. There is complete love in our sin and complete grace for us. And after we experience this love, there is nothing else greater. We are able to love and forgive others. We are able to empathize with others and share in their sin.

Hiding in shame was the only thing holding me back from experiencing freedom. I kept to myself, all the while other women in my life where dealing with the same thing. How many other friends do I have that are struggling in this too? If I shared my shame, would that allow other people to have a me too moment?

The boldness of our story can literally change the lives of the women around us and create a real community of safe, warm, acceptance. I am no longer in shame but free. And I know with certainty, that the next adventures will be scary, bold, even risky. But I can't run from the thought of giving someone else their own me too moment.

"I do not understand the mystery of grace — only that it meets us where we are but does not leave us where it found us."
Anne Lamott

KEY VERSES:
Hosea 2:7-8
Hosea 2:14-15
Psalm 118:5
Matthew 11:28
Hosea 2:19

DISCUSSION QUESTIONS:
+ Are you struggling with shame today? What is something in your life that you are afraid to admit?
+ Has shame ever left you feeling isolated? Misunderstood? Nervous at church and Bible Studies? An outcast among Christians? Why do we let shame drive a wedge between Jesus and us?
+ Shame calls us into isolation and holds us down in the darkness of our sin. Guilt pushes us towards confession and says, "This is not what I have for you." When you mess up, do you earnestly take your sins before the Lord, or do you sweep them under the rug? How can we fight against sitting in our shame and instead let conviction draw us closer to Jesus?
+ Have you allowed someone into your darkness? How does sharing your sins with the people around you bring freedom into your life? How might sharing your shame allow other people to have a me too moment?
+ Madi's counselor shared that the only thing holding her back was that she didn't believe she was worthy. She was questioning God's grace and trying to put it in a formula so it made sense. Do you actually believe you are worthy of God's grace? When you feel like you haven't earned it, how can you let His grace into your life and situations? How can you take a step closer to Him, just as you are?

DEVOTIONALS

CONTRIBUTOR: *Lauren Ann Sklba*

DAY 1

We live in a world of expectations: the grades we strive to earn, the friends we're supposed to keep, the person we aim to be. Good things come when we turn those expectations into goals and foster hope in our hearts. But when we hold on to expectations with tight fists, it's easy for those hopeful standards to turn bitter. Expectations can be traded for experiences that bring letdowns, letdowns that have weight and seem to linger in our souls a little too long. They take on a mind of their own and whisper lies to us. Our hopes that didn't beat the expectation and turned to letdowns transform into shame. And when we hide our shame, we foster it. We let it call our souls a home, and often, we don't even notice this process has taken place.

And then we are put into a new environment where the root of our shame is brought to the surface. When we enter Christian community, it can be difficult to believe we could belong if we've let our shame seep too deep. Shame has a way of isolating us. It convinces us that we are not enough and that we are not lovable. It makes us think those expectations we never met are the same ones the people around us are holding us too, and God isn't any more forgiving.

Shame is a thief. Challenge yourself to stare it in the face and talk it down. Tell your shame that it has no right to set up camp in your spirit. Tell yourself that regardless of your past, of your failures, of your previous mistakes, you are welcome and worthy of love. Because that is what God is telling you, even if His words have been drowned out by the overwhelming whispers of shame.

"Therefore I am now going to allure her; I will lead her into the wilderness and speak tenderly to her. There I will give her back her vineyards, and will make the Valley of Achor a door of hope. There she will respond as in the days of her youth, as in the day she came up out of Egypt."

Hosea 2:14-15

REFLECTION QUESTIONS:

+ Are you struggling with shame today? What is something in your life that you are afraid to admit?

DAY 2

Madi was tempted by the lie that she could not be a part of a community because of her shame. She saw herself surrounded by fellow Christians, but she knew her past. She knew of her own shame. We are quick to see ourselves as half of the others around us because we know the things we've done and we know the things we have failed to do. These thoughts can encourage us to build walls between ourselves and the people that are meant to love us. We abandon grace and pick up comparison. We think of vulnerability as nothing more than a loaded gun ready to take us down. How can we trust these people who are so seemingly perfect?

When we do this we not only isolate ourselves but also begin to hold others to an unrealistic standard for any human. The reality is, no body of believers has it all together. And while we often don't like to confront this reality, when we do, there is freedom and acceptance.

Let us choose vulnerability and see it for what it is: a risky step to take toward being fully known and loved by those we are meant to do life with.

KEY VERSES:
"But if we walk in the light, as he is in the light, we have fellowship with one another, and the blood of Jesus, his Son, purifies us from all sin."
1 John 1:7

REFLECTION QUESTIONS:
+ Has shame ever left you feeling isolated? Misunderstood? Nervous at church and Bible Studies? An outcast among Christians? Why do we let shame drive a wedge between us and Jesus?
+ Have you allowed someone into your darkness? How does sharing your sins with the people around you bring freedom into your life? How might sharing your shame allow other people to have a me too moment?

DAY 3

Madi's counselor told her, "You can't experience freedom if you never accept God's love." When we hold onto shame and isolate ourselves from true community, we also begin to cut ourselves off from God. What begins as hiding from those people around us can quickly translate into hiding from our Father.

It is intimidating, even terrifying, to come before a perfect Father with the areas where we have fallen short. Won't He judge us? Won't He finally see us for who we are, weak and full of mistakes and a less-than-perfect past?

But that's the thing about a perfect Father. We can't comprehend it because we've never experienced it. And when we confess to God the things that are weighing us down, we are greeted with grace. The grace that says "Come home, welcome back, I will always love you. No matter what."

When we avoid confession, we prevent freedom. God does not delight in sin. In fact, He hates it. And when someone He loves is dwelling in sin, He is not pleased. He is heartbroken. When shame and lies cloud our minds and hide His perfect, never-ending, and constant grace, He reaches out to us with wide arms and a warm embrace.

Challenge yourself to sit in silence, to feel those burdens weighing on you. And then invite God into those feelings and ask for the supernatural that only He can grant. The freedom that He loves to grant.

KEY VERSES:
"When hard pressed, I cried to the Lord; he brought me into a spacious place."
Psalm 118:5

REFLECTION QUESTIONS:
+ Shame calls us into isolation and holds us down in the darkness of our sin. Guilt pushes us towards confession and says, "This is not what I have for you." When you mess up, do you earnestly take your sins before the Lord, or do you sweep them under the rug? How can we fight against sitting in our shame and instead, let conviction draw us closer to Jesus?

DAY 4

Grace is not stagnant. God does not give it to us and say, "I am done." No, better yet, He grants us his grace and invites us into a journey of changing our hearts.

Madi struggled to believe her own worth. And when we struggle with loving ourselves, it can be difficult to believe that a perfect God would also be able to love us. But as we invite grace in and embark on a struggle of determination to believe that we are truly so very worthy, we begin to change. We begin to lighten. A burden is lifted, and we can finally run free in the space Jesus has called us into. We can see love overcoming shame.

God's glory is so magnificent and holy that it reaches beyond us. When we experience this goodness personally, it should be hard to contain. When we approach God and rest in his presence, we return beaming with his light. This light is not to be held captive for our own means, but it is to be shared with those around us. As we cast off shame, accept grace, and lean into vulnerability, we are able to not only continue our walk toward freedom but also invite others to come alongside us. When we believe that we are worthy of grace, we can then extend grace to others.

KEY VERSES:
"I will betroth you to me forever; I will betroth you in righteousness and justice, in love and compassion."
Hosea 2:19

REFLECTION QUESTIONS:
+ Madi's counselor shared that the only thing holding her back was that she didn't believe she was worthy. She was questioning God's grace and trying to put it in a formula so it made sense. Do you actually believe you are worthy of God's grace? When you feel like you haven't earned it, how can you let His grace into your life and situations? How can you take a step closer to Him, just as you are?

MORGAN

LIBERTY UNIVERSITY
PROFESSIONAL COMMUNICATION
JUNIOR

Trusting God's Sovereignty

FINDING PEACE IN GOD'S PLAN AND NOT YOUR OWN

If life was a file cabinet and each year was a folder stuffed full of moments and stories and Starbucks receipts, 2015 would be a folder with the words "The Year Things Fell Together" written in big black sharpie across the front. 2015 was a year of trusting the Lord, stepping out in faith, applying and being accepted for a position of ministry leadership at my university, and growing deeply alongside women who have gone from strangers to family. Everything fell together, perfectly.

I've spent the past two semesters in a unique student leadership position at my university, pouring into other leaders spiritually by praying with and for them daily, leading a bible study, meeting with them weekly for times of accountability, and serving them as leaders as much as possible. As I've learned in most areas of ministry, this past year has been the most beautiful mixture of both incredible and just plain hard. I've consumed more coffee than I'm sure is healthy. I've washed more dirty dishes, taken out more trash, and shed more tears than I could have ever imagined at the start of the fall semester. It has been hard work. There have been hard conversations and even harder prayers. My heart has been broken over so many situations, and yet I have felt so near to Christ in fellowship with my sisters.

That was 2015, The Year Things Fell Together. On the folder for year 2016, the words would read a very different sharpied title of "The Year Things Fell Apart."

If I am honest with you, I never thought God would call me away from ministry. Of all the hard and holy things I have expected to come from my walk with Christ, this was never on my radar. I assumed I would continue this ministry of tears and coffee conversations and diving deep into scripture. I love it; my heart aches for it. So when the application process started up, I prayed and didn't feel a significant amount of peace or unrest. I decided to walk through doors as they were opened. I specifically remember praying and telling God that the door would have to be very clearly shut in my face if this was something he didn't want me doing again.

I applied. I interviewed. I waited.

If I am brutally honest, and I feel like I can be brutally honest with you in this space, finding joy in the waiting is very difficult for me. I like structure, black-and-white, yes or no, and waiting is all gray and maybes. In a desperate attempt to appease my restless mind, I refreshed my email about 3,856 times (probably an exaggeration…but maybe not) waiting for that email with a yes-or-no. This, as you can imagine, did nothing for my soul but make me more anxious.

"Wait for the LORD; be strong and take heart and wait for the LORD."
Psalm 27:14

When I arrived back at school, a couple of the girls I had been pouring into excitedly told me they had received their emails and were chosen for the ministry position I was anxiously waiting to hear about. I was excited for them, really I was. I celebrated and rejoiced with them, participating in all the "Oh my gosh! That's incredible!"s and "I'm so excited for you!"s, all the while in the back of my mind wondering why I hadn't received an email like that.

A close friend and mentor of mine gently and quietly asked if I had received an email of rejection (I hadn't), and she encouraged me to make some phone calls. A few days passed with countless conversations that didn't lead anywhere and emails that went unanswered. Finally, I answered the phone to hear the woman I had interviewed with explaining that my application had been misfiled. I wiped tears off my cheeks as she told me that while I was chosen for the position, they offered my spot to another girl by mistake.

"I'm sorry but we can't offer you a spot that someone else has already been offered." I said I understood, and in all the practical ways, I truly did. Mistakes happen, and paperwork can get overwhelming, and there is grace and forgiveness enough for that, freely offered from my end of a phone conversation.

What I didn't understand was where God's hand was in all of that. I didn't understand how His sovereignty tied into such a messy and painful situation. I felt the door shut in my face, but it was more painful than I could have expected. While I wasn't rejected by the leaders who were prayerfully filling positions of leadership, the circumstances of the whole situation were confusing, and the purpose behind it all was nearly impossible to discern.

Later that week as I was driving, I repeated words I've come to memorize.

"Which of you, if your son asks for bread, will give him a stone? Or if he asks for a fish, will give him a snake? If you, then, though you are evil, know how to give good gifts to your children, how much more will your Father in heaven give good gifts to those who ask him!"
Matthew 7:9-11

A year ago, I hesitantly asked God for bread. I shakily offered up my audacious desire like a child holding out a handful of requests. And He gave bread: a position, a difficult and fruitful ministry, a stronger and deeper love for Him, a greater passion for the gospel. I have been blown away by this gift. It has been one of the greatest blessings of my life.

"Every good and perfect gift is from above, coming down from the Father of the heavenly lights, who does not change like shifting shadows."
James 1:17

A month ago, I asked God for bread again, more confident this time. I have had a year of overflowing gifts placed in my hand, and it seems natural and easy to ask for bread again. And it feels as though He has handed me a stone—an unwanted phone call with unwanted news, a stone plopped in my hands cold and hard and covered in dirt.

As I'm writing this, it is such a temptation for me to mask all of this and make you think more highly of me than you should. It would be so easy for me to make the words sound neat and nice or the metaphors light and to band-aid over my own rawness in hopes of portraying my life as something pretty and purposeful. It would be so easy for me to wrap this up in a pretty bow and offer my best hopes for how this next year will turn out. I want to. But I worry the cost of doing that, of portraying my emotions as something they aren't in order to save face, isn't worth the cost of showing you my weaknesses.

In the words of Paul, "Instead, I will boast all the more gladly of my weaknesses so that the power of Christ may rest upon me." Instead, I will bare my cracks and my shortcomings so that the power of the Gospel may shine through.

"But he said to me, "My grace is sufficient for you, for my power is made perfect in weakness." Therefore I will boast all the more gladly about my weaknesses, so that Christ's power may rest on me."
2 Corinthians 12:9

This coming season feels like a stone in my hands when I asked for bread. I have angrily hurled questions at the God of the universe asking if He was deaf to my request, and I have turned inward wondering if there is something I have done to deserve punishment. I made my heart into a legal court, casting blame on God and making my defense. I couldn't understand why I had poured my heart as faithfully as I could into something, and God was taking it away. As Matt Chandler, a pastor at The Village Church in Texas, says, "I put God in my debt," essentially saying that because I had given Him time, service, and love, that He owed me something in return. Paradoxically, at the same time, I was heaping shame on myself, sure that God was taking away my position because I had filled it imperfectly. I was sure that I had made a position an idol in my heart, and God was pulling the rug out from under me as punishment with a laughing "HA!"

Friends, God in His kindness and mercy has gently responded with the Gospel. I am heard. I am seen, and I am loved and cherished in Christ. The wrath that I deserve was fully absorbed by Christ on the cross. This is truth that I am preaching to myself. It is truth that rubs against my heart like gracious, loving sandpaper because it requires me to give up emotions I feel entitled to feel in order to turn toward my Father.

"See what great love the Father has lavished on us, that we should be called children of God! And that is what we are! The reason the world does not know us is that it did not know him."
1 John 3:1

A sweet friend of mine recently sat down with me and listened to my unfiltered emotions while we ate Chipotle. When I was finished, she gently reminded me of the sovereignty of God, and that sometimes God gives us what we couldn't have asked for ourselves.

"But as for me, it is good to be near God. I have made the Sovereign LORD my refuge; I will tell of all your deeds."
Psalm 73:28

I heard that, and I immediately balked at the idea because I am slow to listen and quick to think my own ideas are better. I didn't ask for unfathomable bread. I asked for a specific type of bread in a specific time-frame, and it was not given to me. I don't really know what to do with what He has given me. But as I slowly turn this unfathomable bread over and over in my hands, I am beginning to ask God and to trust Him. My questions have turned to something less accusatory, less self-focused, and more toward questions like, "God, are you revealing an idol in my heart?" and "Are you teaching me what it means to truly find my identity in you rather than in a position of service?"

I think, I hope, this is progress. But the truth is, I don't understand. But what I do know is that He is a good Father, and He gives good gifts to his children. I can't picture this next year, but I know that God's goodness can and will be in it. What looks and feels like a stone to me may be the mercy of God in giving me a greater gift, unfathomable as it is. Perhaps what I was asking for was a stone, and He is graciously giving bread better than I could have asked for myself.

KEY VERSES:

Psalm 27:14
Matthew 7:9-11
James 1:17
2 Corinthians 12:9
1 John 3:1
Psalm 73:28

DISCUSSION QUESTIONS:

+ What scares you most about the unknown? How do you find yourself responding when you are in times of waiting?

+ Morgan explains that through her disappointment she became angry with God, throwing questions and frustration at Him, wondering if there was something she did to deserve this. Can you relate to Morgan's frustration? When you don't understand what He is doing or why things have turned out a certain way, how can you begin to lean into Him for more understanding?

+ Sometimes God gives you what you couldn't have asked for yourself. Think back on a time in your life when you felt like you deserved bread but got a stone instead. Looking at it now, can you see purpose in God's plan?

+ Have you ever felt like God owed you something because of the service, time, and efforts you've given to Him? How can we be followers of Christ that continuously give ourselves away without expecting anything in return?

+ How can you turn away from prayers and questions that are accusatory and self-focused, and instead open your eyes to how he's leading you? How might this change your perspective?

DEVOTIONALS

DEVOTIONAL CONTRIBUTOR: *Rachel Holland*

DAY 1

When God calls us into the unknown, we can so easily become engulfed in fear, anxiety, and confusion. Morgan talks about how she never thought God would call her away from ministry, something she loved the most. This new season she was approaching was not on her radar. So often we are told that we must always serve in the church, that we must always lead others to Christ in some way. Although this is true, there are seasons of waiting where God takes us out to mold, shape, and plant his image on us, so that He can bring us back into our calling. Throughout the gospels it often mentions that Jesus went to a solitary place, or that he withdrew and went into the wilderness. He stepped out of His ministry into a solitary place, spent time with the Father, and from these moments in the wilderness came moments of miraculous healing, restoration and good news throughout His incredible ministry on Earth.

This season of waiting could look spiritually dry, lonely, anxious, or even desperate. Christine Caine refers this season as a photographer's dark room. Although the room is dark, it is the place where an image is being transformed onto canvas to create a beautiful masterpiece. Just as Jesus takes us out of seasons and into uncertainty, we can be sure that he is molding and transforming us, to make a masterpiece.

KEY VERSES:
"And we all, who with unveiled faces contemplate the Lord's glory, are being transformed into his image with ever-increasing glory, which comes from the Lord, who is the Spirit."
2 Corinthians 3:18

REFLECTION QUESTIONS:
+ What scares you most about the unknown? How do you find yourself responding when you are in times of waiting?

Morgan mentions that her coming season feels like a stone in her hands instead of the bread she asked for. So many times we feel this way about what the Lord puts in our path. We dream about and envision one thing, and then He gives us something completely different. Morgan talks about how she began to question the Lord, and wonder what she must have done to receive this punishment. Can you relate to this? Our view of God can become miscued when we don't understand His plan, timing, or the circumstances that He places in front of us. Although He is a good, good father, we may not see Him as that during this time.

The Bible mentions how the lilies of the valley do not work or spin, yet the Father makes them beautiful. And the birds do not sow or reap, yet the Father feeds them. What a beautiful picture of our Father who provides for every single living thing. Yet so often we doubt that He will provide for us, His precious treasures. Morgan didn't see the outcome from not getting the position she desperately desired, but she held onto the promise that the Lord gives good gifts to His children far better than we could ever imagine.

KEY VERSES:
"Look at the birds of the air; they do not sow or reap or store away in barns, and yet your heavenly Father feeds them. Are you not much more valuable than they? Can any one of you by worrying add a single hour to your life?"
Matthew 6:26-27

"Which of you, if your son asks for bread, will give him a stone? Or if he asks for a fish, will give him a snake? If you, then, though you are evil, know how to give good gifts to your children, how much more will your Father in heaven give good gifts to those who ask him!"
Matthew 7:9-11

REFLECTION QUESTIONS:

+ Morgan explains that through her disappointment she became angry with God, throwing questions and frustration at Him, wondering if there was something she did to deserve this. Can you relate to Morgan's frustration? When you don't understand what He is doing or why things have turned out a certain way, how can you begin to lean into Him for more understanding?

+ Sometimes God gives you what you couldn't have asked for yourself. Think back on a time in your life when you felt like you deserved bread but got a stone instead. Looking at it now, can you see purpose in God's plan?

DAY 3

Morgan writes how she couldn't understand why she had poured her heart as faithfully into something, and God was taking it away. She mentions how she was sure that this closed door was because she hadn't done a good job, and that God was taking the position away from her because of it. When things don't go the way that we planned, we begin to question God. We question His presence, His sovereignty, and we may even question His being. Or maybe we're on the opposite side, and we feel like God owes us something for our hard work, dedication, and commitment, yet we don't feel known, loved, or valued.

Regardless of these two sides, the Father's love is infinite for us. His love is deep, His love is wide, and His love is vast. Like Morgan said, she didn't understand why the door closed, but she trusted it was act of mercy from the heavenly father. The truth is, God knows us far better than we know ourselves. He knows the number of hairs on our heads, and every thought we have before we have them. He knows us, and He loves us. He knows exactly what we need, and exactly what we don't. This overwhelming gracious love alone is enough to trust Him and His plan. It is enough to keep pouring into areas in our life even if we never receive anything in return. It is enough to be still and know that He is God.

KEY VERSES:
"He says, "Be still, and know that I am God."
Psalm 46:10a

"Many are the plans in a person's heart, but it is the LORD's purpose that prevails."
Proverbs 19:21

REFLECTION QUESTIONS:
+ Have you ever felt like God owed you something because of the service, time, and efforts you've given to Him? How can we be followers of Christ that continuously give ourselves away without expecting anything in return?

DAY 4

Morgan mentions that it was very difficult to find joy in the waiting for an answer. She talks about refreshing her email, only to make her even more anxious. Can you relate to this? Is there something you have been waiting for? Maybe weeks, months, or maybe you have been waiting years for an answer. Waiting calls for patience, and often times, we can wind up feeling impatient, eager, and frustrated to get the answer God has designed for us. When this happens our prayers can begin to become self-focused, we want answers now and in our time. We must trust that the Lord is up to something, and He will reveal it in His timing.

In a world where we can find answers to almost anything with one click, thanks to our Google App on our smartphones, it can be extremely difficult to wait on an answer that is unseen. Finding joy and peace during these times is no doubt, extremely difficult, as it is a constant struggle to sit in God's present sovereignty. However, the Bible says to be strong, take courage, and wait for the Lord. Be strong. Take courage. These are choices that we can make each day while we are waiting for an answer from the Lord. This doesn't mean that each day we have to force a smile on our face in the midst of our impatience, but rather we can smile because we know our Heavenly Father has a perfect answer for a perfect time.

KEY VERSES:
"I remain confident of this: I will see the goodness of the Lord in the land of the living. Wait for the LORD; be strong and take heart and wait for the Lord."
Psalm 27:13-14

"But if we hope for what we do not yet have, we wait for it patiently"
Romans 8:25

REFLECTION QUESTIONS:
+ How can you turn away from prayers and questions that are accusatory and self-focused, and instead open your eyes to how He's leading you? How might this change your perspective?

Act of Surrender

FINDING BALANCE BETWEEN SERVING AND SITTING AT HIS FEET

I'm a firm believer in the power of story. Tell me what's shaped you and broken you and made you the person you are. Talk to me about what you love, what makes your eyes sparkle with passion and sets your heart ablaze. I love to hear about the darkest valleys, the moments that seemed unconquerable before the level ground was reached.

Stories are powerful because they hold the key to our lives, but I'm learning that stories, our stories as we try to create them, are powerless. I'm discovering that this life is not my story to tell. It's God's story, and I am just the vessel.

Over the course of my college career, it's been so easy for me to get caught up in what I'm accomplishing for the Gospel. My campus is a place that isn't saturated with the love of God, and before even starting college, my intention was to be a light-bearer and flood my campus with the love of Christ. This was the Great Commission, right? Live out the Gospel to all people? My heart was fed and nourished during my first year as I became involved in a couple of campus ministries. God crossed my path with a fantastic group of unique and passionate people who also desired to make God's name known on campus, and we started building an intentional community based on gathering and growing together. It was a fruitful season, and I sit back now and see how much the hand of God was so vividly at work.

"May the Lord make your love increase and overflow for each other and for everyone else, just as ours does for you. May he strengthen your hearts so that you will be blameless and holy in the presence of our God and Father when our Lord Jesus comes with all his holy ones."
1 Thessalonians 3:12-13

It's funny how quickly things can change. That same first year of college ended in the spring with a lot of transition. There had been some conflict in my community, a core member of my friend group was transferring to a different school, my summer internship plans were a mess, and I was working towards graduating a year early, which meant extra stress and additional planning as a freshman. Instead of allowing these minor trials to push me towards God, I let them draw my focus away from Him and towards my temporary circumstances and how I could fix them. Over the summer, I went through a period where I felt like I wasn't "doing" enough for the Gospel. I went to church every Sunday. Yes. I read my Bible every morning before going to work. Great. Sometimes I talked about my faith at work. Fantastic. I was missing significance and flashy events instead of seeing that time as a season where God wanted to grow me. I thought the solution to what I thought was stagnation would be for me to hit the ground running during the next school year and get my Gospel on.

I abide by the saying, "Go big or stay home." This goes for eating cookies, planning events, and apparently serving Christ. That year, I took on leadership with two campus ministries along with attending two others. My class schedule was crazy, but I wanted to stay invested in my community, so I could often be found with my face in my phone texting three different people to organize something or plan a time to meet. I would sit at lunch in between classes and mentally rehearse my schedule in my head, making sure I was ready for what was next. I was working so hard to form a story of significance, but I was missing the point. The focus became on what I was doing and what I was accomplishing and how I was bringing God to campus . . . Obviously, there was a lot of "I" involved. I often looked back to the previous summer and thought to myself, "Dang, I've come a long way," yet something was off as my heart began to harden.

My goal of "doing" more for God and His people was accomplished, but my frustration and stress grew as I tried so hard to take care of everything that I missed the purpose. I would be so focused on what was next that I wasn't appreciating where I was and what God had for me in that present moment. I was so overcome with the desire to take care of everything to the point that I was missing grace. My heart thriving is not the most important thing; however, if my heart is hardened by a need to do it all, it's not operating from a place of lavished grace and love, making all my efforts futile. I so desperately wanted to help others thrive, even though I myself was not.

Thankfully, God doesn't leave His children struggling, even when they're fighting so stubbornly to do their thing without any help. I've always been that kid, the I-can-take-care-of-this-but-thanks-for-offering poster child, but I have a graciously persistent Father.

All of this eventually came full circle. During the winter semester of my second year, I found myself in a place often defined as rock bottom. I had gotten used to family members and friends giving me the "Wow, you're so busy. I don't know how you do it" speech, which I had worn like a badge of honor the entire year. But as I so fiercely tried to write my story to see how much I could accomplish in my short time in college, I was left with a feeling of emptiness and crippling anxiety like never before as I lived with the fear that I couldn't do enough. My time with God became nonexistent. My faith began to crumble, and I was weighed down by an unexplainable heaviness. My story became mere words as I missed the heavenly meaning and eternal purpose while I rushed to fulfill everything and take care of everyone under the guise of bearing God's light. God is moving, but it's crazy how I miss it when I take matters into my own hands.

"For it is by grace you have been saved, through faith—and this is not from yourselves, it is the gift of God— not by works, so that no one can boast. For we are God's handiwork, created in Christ Jesus to do good works, which God prepared in advance for us to do."
Ephesians 2:8-10

One of my mentors is a good family friend of my grandparents'. Even though he's halfway through his seventies, he's the hardest worker both for the Gospel and in his career that I know, but he has a peace and contentment in God that's unexplainable. In one of our phone calls where I was word exploding about all that I had on my plate and everything I was trying to do, I could almost hear him shaking his head over the line. His voice was soft and understanding, and I'll never forget him saying, "Sydney, you are not created to be a human doing. You are created as a human being. Only when you grasp that can you fulfill the work of the Lord."

This gentle call-out showed me that something was off, that I had it wrong. Yes, I had all the head knowledge, accolades, ceaseless efforts, and good works for following Christ, but my heart wasn't where it needed to be. I was too caught up in building this great image of being a Christ-follower instead of actually getting down to the nitty-gritty of living out the Gospel, of being in God's grace. I was focused so much on who I am and what I was doing instead of focusing on who God is and how He is so beautifully moving.

"You who are trying to be justified by the law have been alienated from Christ; you have fallen away from grace."
Galatians 5:4

As daughters of God, we are called to flourish. We're called to see this life through a divine lens as God paints His picture of redemption. We're called to serve Him. But we absolutely cannot do that if we're rooting and grounding our efforts to glorify Him IN ourselves. We can't stay in a place of thinking that we're the best versions of ourselves as we cling to old, law-like ways and miss His grace. The only way we can thrive in God is if we're remaining and resting in Him, bearing fruit, and moving as He calls us.

"I am the vine; you are the branches. If you remain in me and I in you, you will bear much fruit; apart from me you can do nothing. If you do not remain in me, you are like a branch that is thrown away and withers; such branches are picked up, thrown into the fire and burned."
John 15:5-6

Jesus is the vine. He's the center. He's the foundation. We are just the branches, which means we can do absolutely nothing without the vine. We receive our very being from Him, the direction of our growth from Him, the chance to prosper from Him. Only in Him can we bear fruit. Just as the verses in John 15 say, if we don't remain in Him, we're put through the fire, and we fail to bear fruit. I began to realize that this was what had happened to my faith. Without remaining in Christ, I was falling apart even though I thought I was doing good work.

"Flourish" is one of my absolute favorite words. Flourishing is life giving. It promises abundance and fullness, but in order to flourish and in order to bear fruit, we have to place ourselves in a favorable environment to grow. It's exactly what life is like when you're clinging to the love of Jesus, when you place your being in Him. In this season, flourishing means taking time aside from the demands of this world to sit at His feet. If my actions are designed for bringing glory to God, His attributes should be evident in my life. However, the traits and goodness of God can't be revealed through my life if I don't spend precious time seeking My Father and learning Who He is above all of my earthly efforts to serve Him.

"Immediately Jesus made the disciples get into the boat and go on ahead of him to the other side, while he dismissed the crowd. After he had dismissed them, he went up on a mountainside by himself to pray. Later that night, he was there alone."
Matthew 14:22-23

There are multiple moments in the Bible where Jesus Himself takes time away from the crowds to meet His Father. In Matthew 14, Jesus performs the miracle of feeding the five thousand, but afterwards, He does something that comes across as unusual in today's rushed world—He sends the people away, exits the party, and goes to a mountainside by Himself to pray. Jesus has just fulfilled this amazing work of God, yet He removes Himself to refocus. Matthew doesn't mention what Jesus talked to God about on the mountain, but it reveals that He needed time to abide just like we do. Jesus needed His next steps, which I think is amazing considering the following verses in Matthew 14 are about Jesus walking on the water. I can't help but wonder if that time Jesus spent alone with God on the mountaintop is what equipped Him to do His next astounding miracle. It seems that, like us, Jesus could do His best work when He spent time at the feet of His Abba, when the focus was on God alone. Not the people. Not the work. Only God and His glory.

In looking at this example of Jesus taking a step back from the crowd, I began to learn where flourishing begins for me in this new season. I knew that God was telling me to take a slight step back in order to shift the focus from me to Him where it should have been all along. Soon after that original conversation with my mentor, my boyfriend and I sat at lunch where I was listing out everything I had to do that week and how I didn't think I could accomplish everything. My guy put down his pizza (big deal), looked me in the eyes, and politely said: "You need to learn three words, Syd: No, relax, and content." As much as I hated to admit it, I realized he was right—heck, he stopped eating to offer those words of wisdom.

Through these three small words, God began teaching me about what it meant to truly flourish.

To say no means to decline what distracts me from the glory of God. No to this life being about me. No to the idolatry that puts good deeds above

God Himself. No to feeling like it's my calling to do everything without any help or reliance on others. No to demands that distract me from the deeper purpose of fulfilling God's work. Saying no leaves room for saying yes to what is better, which always surrounds God becoming greater.

Learning to relax has taught me to appreciate this journey more as I make time for worshipping in the everyday. For me, this means taking conscious time away from the busyness and need to do it all in order to make sure my heart is in the right place. Though I'm still involved in all of my campus ministries, this might mean taking an evening off to recharge. Sometimes it requires dwindling a day of three events down to one. It involves releasing the fear of letting people down and being honest with others about why I'm stepping back. The benefit is the heart nourishing that comes from spending time in His Word as I make intentional time for Him and the joy that comes from being present in one place with one focus.

The last word—content—is probably the most difficult for me. This is the one I'm still learning. God keeps revealing that this is the season to "be," to learn what it means to abide and remain in Him only. He's teaching me how to be the branches, to not get too caught up in the action of what's going on in my life right now, but to slow down and simply walk alongside Him and to be thankful in that instead of wishing He had me someplace different.

These three words have been focus shifters, allowing me to see this life through His lens, revealing that God wants to offer me abundant, flourishing life, but the key to that is learning that this is not my story.

"The thief comes only to steal and kill and destroy; I have come that they may have life, and have it to the full."
John 10:10

Taking a step back and learning to abide wasn't easy, and at times, it can still feel like admitting defeat as I face the fear of disappointing others or not living up to an immeasurable standard I set for myself. In those moments, God continuously reminds me that sometimes it takes letting go of what seems to be good to receive what's best. Jesus didn't fulfill the work of God out of some need to perform or to live up to any expectations other than His Father's. As I give up the idea that it's my responsibility to do everything, God reveals the heavenly perspective that

I need in order to keep Him as the focus as I seek to declare His name. When I remain in God and allow Him to do the work, I can live with peace in my heart that what I do or don't do is not what truly matters. It's about His holiness being adored at all times, in rest, in work, and in all the moments in between.

As someone who has lived much of her life stressed out and terrified that everything will combust into flames if she's not directly involved, this new mindset is freeing. When I hand over the story to Him, it releases the shackles of stress and defeat that arose when I made the Gospel about me and allows me to drink deep of the fullness of life that He offers.

The pressure is off if we're dwelling in His love. It's become so clear that I've tried to make this life my story, and I fail at writing it every single time. This is not my story. It's His, and I've complicated this issue for far too long. My white-knuckled grip on the pen, despite my efforts still being to make Him known, have only left me with dried-out ink and ripped pages. It's time to hand it over, to find myself at His feet again before I take another step. It's time to make this story His again.

KEY VERSES:
1 Thessalonians 3:12-13
Ephesians 2:8-10
Galatians 5:4
John 15:5-6
Matthew 14:22-23
John 10:10

DISCUSSION QUESTIONS:
+ Where are some places in your life that you feel the need to "do it all"? What are difficulties you face trying to accomplish this?
+ Do you find yourself losing focus or passion for Christ when the patterns of life seem normal? Why is it sometimes difficult to serve the Lord in the mundane? Instead of craving flashy events or spiritual highs, how can we stay faithful and focused in the less exciting seasons?
+ Sydney shares how she was working so hard to form a story of significance that she began to make it about herself. When serving God, is it easy to make your efforts to glorify Him about you? Is there something in your life that you're doing to bolster your image rather than as a way to serve God? How can you catch yourself in the act of doing this?
+ Sometimes we get so caught up in doing things for God and being a good Christian, that we forget to rest in Him. Are there things in your life that you need to take a step back from in order to reset and return the focus to God? What does abiding and remaining in God mean to you? Where is the balance between serving and sitting at His feet?
+ If you're being honest with yourself, who or what is controlling your story? Is it you? Your boyfriend? Your parents? Your ambitions? Your pride? How can you loosen your grip on the pen and begin to let Christ write your story?

DEVOTIONALS

CONTRIBUTOR: *Alicia Dalee*

DAY 1

As humans, we are all called to a purpose. We are created in the image of a creator and as His creation called to specific positions throughout life in the communities He has placed us. But the Lord calls us to specific positions throughout life — the keyword being life. He does not call us to specific positions today. He does not call us to accomplish all of the positions He has laid out for us at once. He gives us a lifetime to accomplish the roles in which he created us to fill. Sydney tells the story of a girl who took on one too many positions— all good. But, instead of placing her trust in her Savior to fill the positions of her community she attempted to spearhead more roles than she as individual could take on single-handedly. In the midst of her attempt to serve in everything, she began the slow decent in a wick without any wax to fuel her fire.

But a heart at rest is a heart that trusts. A heart that trusts is a heart that abides in its savior to sustain it. When Sydney focused her time on the one thing that counts, Jesus, she found a healed heart and gained the mental energy to serve in the position suited for her, not every positioned offered to her.

When we attempt to serve in roles without prayerfully considering if the roles are for us it leaves our hearts burnt-out, confused and tired. What would it look like for you to spur on other believers to take on your roles? What would it look like to allow others the seat at the head of the table? Have you taken the time to ask yourself why you are serving in the roles you are? Is it for the title, the approval, or is it to serve His people? Are you serving with a humble heart or for the prestige of recognition?

KEY VERSES:
"As a prisoner for the Lord, then, I urge you to live a life worthy of the calling you have received. Be completely humble and gentle; be patient, bearing with one another in love. Make every effort to keep the unity of the Spirit through the bond of peace."
Ephesians 4:1-3

REFLECTION QUESTIONS:
+ Where are some places in your life that you feel the need to "do it all"? What are difficulties you face trying to accomplish this?

DAY 2

Like Sydney, we often take on one too many roles from faithful hearts that genuinely want to serve the King. However, if we look at the call to discipleship that Jesus gives us in Matthew 28 we see a call that urges us to teach others the lessons that Jesus has taught us. Jesus is faithful to discipline and guide us in order that we can serve and better love His brothers and sisters; we are His co-heirs. As we teach and serve others we equip fellow to believers to be disciples alongside us. As we see our calling through this lens, it empowers us to relinquish our roles and allow fellow disciples to serve in our place. When we allow others to serve alongside us we begin to see what Jesus meant when He said we are one body with many members, we see a true picture of biblical community.

Before we take a look at how to seek true rest in Jesus, first take a look at the messy, busy heart within you, and within me. Ask yourself at the root, truly, where can you relinquish a duty? Are you mentoring a younger girl with a heart for serving others? What would it look like to offer her the leadership role you honestly, simply, don't have time for? What would it look like to relinquish the bind of self-image and empower God's people? Can you think of a time in your life when you served in too many roles? If you are honest with yourself, right now, today, are you worn out? What would it look like to empower a fellow sister to lead and serve?

Paul's words to Timothy say, "For the Spirit God gave us does not make us timid, but gives us power, love and self-discipline." Paul empowered Timothy to go and serve God's kingdom. Paul did not try to take the glory and carry on Timothy's role as well. He urged Timothy to continue to preach the gospel.

KEY VERSES:
"Therefore go and make disciples of all nations, baptizing them in the name of the Father and of the Son and of the Holy Spirit, and teaching them to obey everything I have commanded you. And surely I am with you always, to the very end of the age."
Matthew 28:19-20

REFLECTION QUESTIONS:

+ Sydney shares how she was working so hard to form a story of significance that she began to make it about herself. When serving God, is it easy to make your efforts to glorify Him about you? Is there something in your life that you're doing to bolster your image rather than as a way to serve God? How can you catch yourself in the act of doing this?

DAY 3

It humbles a heart to realize we have a Savior who is not interested merely in our service but also in our hearts. Jesus cares for the state of your soul. He understands we are human, finite, often weak, easily tired, and instead of asking us to serve more, do more, be more, He simply says, "Come to me all who are weary and burdened, and I will give you rest." It is an empathy that leads us to repentance. We have a Savior that understands our wearied minds, our tired bodies, and out of His goodness offers us to come to Him and find rest. He asks us to come away with Him and rest.

We are called to service, but we are also called to rest. In the business of life, it is easy to buy into the do more culture. We are so busy? But, busy with what? The most important thing calls you to Him to rest. This goes against the grain of American culture.

Jesus desires to talk to you. He desires to hear your momentary thoughts. He desires to know you fully. Do you ever feel at the end of the day you scarcely have time for Jesus? Take 10 seconds and ask yourself a very honest question, how is your heart? At this moment is it resting in Jesus? Or like Sydney, are you tired? Are you worn out?

If the answer is yes, what would it look like for you to get away with Jesus and allow Him to give you rest?

Read Matthew 11:28-29— notice the word 'learn.' In order to learn we must first rest, and to best serve for Him we must first gain the knowledge of his word and learn to abide with His spirit.

KEY VERSES:
"Come to me, all you who are weary and burdened, and I will give you rest. Take my yoke upon you and learn from me, for I am gentle and humble in heart, and you will find rest for your souls."
Matthew 11:28-29

REFLECTION QUESTIONS:
+ Sometimes we get so caught up in doing things for God and being a good Christian, that we forget to rest in Him. Are there things in your life that you need to take a step back from in order to reset and return the focus to God? What does abiding and remaining in God mean to you? Where is the balance between serving and sitting at His feet?

Sydney shares how stories are a powerful thing. It's the reason that we're all fascinated with the latest blockbuster film, Netflix series, or Nicholas Sparks book. We want to know what happens next: who falls in love with who, who lives, who dies, how does the story end? It's the thing that convinces us to click "Next Episode Playing in 15 Seconds" every single time, even when it's 2am and have to be up for class in 6 hours.

The stories we tell with our lives hold even more power. God wants to use our stories to spread His love all over this world, to every nook and cranny that we never imagined we could go. But the truth of the matter is our stories lose all significance when we try to take control and write our own ending. Our lives are God's story, and we are simply His vessels.

What story are you telling with your life? Who is writing your story? Is it you or the people around you? Are you letting your need for perfection or attention write this chapter? Is your fear of losing that person dominating this page of your life? We have to realize who or what we're letting control our story and daily hand the pen back to God. The pressure is off when we're dwelling in His love and thinking about the entire story rather than the current page we're on. Today, hand your story over to the greatest Author of all time.

KEY VERSES:
"Many are the plans in a person's heart, but it is the Lord's purpose that prevails."
Proverbs 19:21

REFLECTION QUESTIONS:
+ If you're being honest with yourself, who or what is controlling your story? Is it you? Your boyfriend? Your parents? Your ambitions? Your pride? How can you loosen your grip on the pen and begin to let Christ write your story?

ANDREA

APPALACHIAN STATE UNIVERSITY
SOCIAL WORK
JUNIOR

Never Losing Faith

LEANING IN CLOSER TO CHRIST WHEN LIFE GETS TOUGH

We are constantly told the same clichés: *Life is short. Cherish every moment. Tell your friends and family that you love them everyday.* Despite these reminders, we often fail to live life like the gift it truly is. We tend to dwell on the difficulties of the insignificant. We tend to worry about the future. We tend to get angry at our loved ones for things that won't even matter tomorrow. Here's another cliché for you: *we don't know the treasures we have until they're gone.*

July 2015. My mom was diagnosed with peritoneal cancer. Stage Four. A lot of tears were shed. My mom and family had no idea that the pain she was experiencing in her side was anything even close to being something to seriously worry about. But the CT scan revealing the masses taking over her abdomen proved otherwise. We asked the doctors what we needed to do to fight the powerful, yet malevolent, cells attacking my mom's body. This only seemed like the next logical step. We needed to form a defense and do everything we could to help my mom beat this disease.

We were lucky enough to live a short 35-minute drive from Wake Forest Baptist Medical Center, a nationally-ranked hospital in cancer care. And my mom's doctors definitely upheld the titles their hospital earned. They assured us that they would do everything in their power to help my mom win her battle against cancer. Their plan consisted of two-hour chemotherapy treatments that she would undergo every two weeks. This would be followed by a 48-hour treatment she would take at home. The whole time, my mom was reminding us to keep praying. I tried. But studying my Bible was hard. How could a God who was supposed to be merciful place this disease in my mom? But I tried. Because reading verses that displayed God's love and sharing those verses with my mom helped to provide some hope, even if it was fleeting. The bigger problem, the reason I was tremendously upset, had to do with the fact that this was not my mom's first fight with cancer.

In 2009, she was diagnosed with breast cancer. Stage One. She underwent a lumpectomy and radiation treatments and won that battle. No matter what stage cancer is found in, however, these battles are never easily won. These cells know how to wear down the physical body, which then wear down the mind and the emotions. Cancer treatments take their own toll on a person. But we hope the treatments are there for the greater good, unlike the cells. Radiation treatments took a lot out of my mom. But the cells were defeated. They backed away. And we rejoiced. All the hard parts worked together for the greater good.

When my mom heard her second diagnosis of cancer, she admitted that she would need time to think about whether or not she wanted to put herself through chemotherapy. The masses were already placing a heavy pain on her body, so would she want to place even more pain on herself? But the doctors had their plan. And they were confident in their plan. And to calm my mom's racing thoughts, they informed us that the type of chemotherapy they would have her undergo would have minimal side effects on her body. So she decided to give it a chance. She did those two-hour treatments. She did those 48-hour treatments. And the next CT scan she underwent showed that the masses were shrinking. We had every reason to believe we could be hopeful.

During these months, I didn't try to get any closer to God. My anger at the situation had weakened my relationship with Him, and I didn't even realize it. I was placing my faith in the medicine, the doctors. I wanted them to fix this. Then everything would be okay. It was only every once in a while that I would turn to God and ask Him to continue the progress my mom was experiencing. It was the least He could do, right?

"Your word is a lamp for my feet, a light on my path."
Psalm 119:105

November 5, 2015. All of my mom's treatments, CT scans, and doctor appointments were leading to this day. She would undergo a twelve-hour surgery where the surgeons would work to remove the remaining cells finding an unwelcomed home in her abdomen. My mom's surgeon was kind. He was friendly. He was the best at his job. We were still hopeful. Everything was going to be okay.

6 a.m. My mom was taken down to surgery. We were given time to spend as a family. We sat around her. We held hands. We cried. We prayed.

My mom was so close to winning this battle. The past few months had been mostly good. I asked God, "You placed this hardship in my mom's life. But you have blessed the situation. Please just give my mom's body the strength to defeat this final obstacle. Please just give the doctors the knowledge and energy they need. Please turn this into something better." We said our final 'I love you's,' we said our final blessings, we said our final 'I'll see you soon's.' And she was taken into surgery.

All my family and I could do now was wait. We sat in the waiting room, keeping ourselves and our minds occupied. We received updates every two hours, being told my mom was doing well, so well. I didn't bother spending time with God and in the Word while waiting. Instead, I did everything I could to distract myself from the situation entirely. Everything was going to be okay. It was about halfway through, 12 p.m., when the lead surgeon came out to speak to us. That was not a good sign.

My mom was alive. She was OK. But the procedure had to be cut short. He took out as much of each of the masses as he could without affecting any major organs. Flooding my mother's abdomen with heated chemotherapy was a major part of the procedure; that would have gotten rid of masses they couldn't take out by hand and any remaining spots of malicious cells. He never did that during my mom's procedure. The cancer was too far along. The cells were too aggressive. He could only remove about 75 percent. We now only had two ideal options: my mom could undergo more chemotherapy treatments and try to take some control over the cancer. or she could leave her body alone and just try to handle the pain the cells were causing. Of course, he had to let us know the truth about the situation, something a CT scan couldn't tell us. Seeing with his own eyes and feeling with his own hands how aggressive these cells were, he was not confident that they could gain significant control of this disease. At best, he gave my mom 18 months left on this earth.

Tears. Lots of tears. I broke down in sobs in the middle of the waiting room. I sat in my sadness for 20 minutes, trying to muster any sort of composure. My dad and my brother sat with me. We sat with our heads in our hands. It was if the world around us froze. Total silence. And in that moment, I truly knew what absolute heartbreak felt like. No person should know what that feels like.

But we had to figure out the next step. That was going up to the room where they took my mom and being with her. It took her awhile to wake up from the anesthesia. And when she did, she was groggy and tired. She still underwent a major surgery. She needed rest. But we sat with her for a few hours. We sat together as a family and held her hands. Blowing her kisses when she managed to open her eyes, even if just for a few seconds. We decided to let her sleep through the night. We let her doctors know that we wanted to be the ones to tell her the news. She needed to hear it from us.

I'll never forget the first thing she told me and my brother after we told her, the way she looked us right in our eyes as we sat next to her and held her hands: "I'm not mad at God." It was the first time God entered my mind all day. I thought to myself, How could you not be mad at God? He put you through this mess, through this evil disease. He gave you hope that you would be healed. And then He reveals that the whole situation was worse than we could imagine. How could He take you away from me, Mom? That's not fair.

"Consider it pure joy, my brothers and sisters, whenever you face trials of many kinds, because you know that the testing of your faith produces perseverance. Let perseverance finish its work so that you may be mature and complete, not lacking anything."
James 1:2-4

And that was that. All I was concerned about was making sure you could be taken home as soon as possible. We all just wanted to reassure you that you could have all the time needed to weigh the option of undergoing chemotherapy again or not. We all just wanted to reassure you that the decision was up to you and only you. We wanted you to be comfortable.

The hour-and-45-minute drive back to school three days later was one of the hardest things I've ever had to do. I didn't know how to be away from my family at a time like this. But during that drive, I saw one of the most beautiful sunsets I had ever seen. I saw the colors in the sky change into bright oranges and soft pinks as Ben Rector's "When a Heart Breaks" played in the background.

This isn't easy. This isn't clear. And you don't need Jesus until you're here.

This was not easy. And this definitely was not clear. I was utterly angry with God for placing this new hardship in my mom's life. She had already faced so many hardships. My dad had already faced so many hardships.

My brother and I had already faced enough hardships of our own. Why this? Why bring us this pain? The anger and sadness and disappointment in my head clouded all of the other emotions. I didn't know how I could possibly feel anything other than anger and sadness. It was numbing.

I let friends know of what had happened. They let me know that they would be praying for me. They constantly let me know that they were thinking of me and my mom and my family, constantly praying for us. I was so mad at God for having this be part of His plan, the plan I am always told is perfect. But when people always asked me how my mom was doing and told me that they were always praying without me having to ask, it got me thinking.

In the months between July and November, when I gathered up the courage to plead to God, praying to Him, "Please keep my mom with You. Please place Your healing hands on her." During those months, it was hard to place trust in God. I placed more trust in science. Ultimately, though, we could never know what exactly would happen. Only God knew. It was all up to God.

After that November day, I was angry. I was frustrated. But I had no idea what else to do. While friends were being supportive, the encouragements they were offering weren't truly affecting my heart. I thought, *Maybe God would be able to prove something good. Maybe He has something nice to say.* It was hard and it was hard to find motivation, but I decided to dedicate each morning to a devotional, starting my day with learning about the life of Jesus, hoping it might affect how I would go about my day.

After so many tears were shed, after so many discussions with my mom, my dad, and my brother, after so many plans were listed by doctors, I was still feeling emotionally drained. I was not strong enough for this. My family was leaning on each other, but I felt absolutely weak. It was then that I realized I had nowhere else to turn. Except for the power and the love and the strength of the Lord.

I thought I knew what the life, death, and resurrection of Jesus did for God's children, but as the song that played during that sunset proved, I had no idea how badly I needed Jesus until I was placed right in this part of His will. In dedicating more of my time to being in the Word, I slowly comprehended the fact that begging for more of God, more of His strength and His love, was what I needed to be doing from the very beginning. I came to the realization that this is why God, the entity of all that is good, places bad in our paths: to feel an absolute need for Him, to see that His love still showers over us.

"In all this you greatly rejoice, though now for a little while you may have had to suffer grief in all kinds of trials. These have come so that the proven genuineness of your faith—of greater worth than gold, which perishes even though refined by fire—may result in praise, glory and honor when Jesus Christ is revealed."
1 Peter 1:6-7

Just like my mom's first conquer over cancer, where all those parts of treatments came together for the greater good of the health of my mom, so did the parts of the life of Jesus come together for the goodness that the Lord would place in our lives.

Just like the battle my mom now faces each day of her life, Jesus fought the greatest battle of all: total abandonment from the Father. Jesus already took on the worst. Jesus already took on pain. He knows how we feel when we face our trials and He feels it on a level we could never imagine. And He knows why we feel it. He knows that we get mad and frustrated and confused and disheartened. But He calls us to love Him.

Life is short. That is indeed true. But this life in the physical world is nothing compared to the eternal life we'll get to live with Jesus in Heaven. Christ experienced complete separation from God, so that we won't ever have to feel so alone. Instead, we'll get to experience deep love with Him, a love we should share with our family and friends, cherishing the moments we are granted with them—moments centered in Christ. If Christ is indeed at the center of our relationships, then we'll be able to understand just how wonderful those relationships are all through the grace of God. And when death forces us to be separated from our loved ones, we can continue sharing that grace with those still around us, knowing that our loved ones are experiencing a love so immense and so deep with the Lord in Heaven.

"Because we have heard of your faith in Christ Jesus and of the love you have for all God's people— the faith and love that spring from the hope stored up for you in heaven and about which you have already heard in the true message of the gospel that has come to you."
Colossians 1:4-6a

In knowing that Jesus feels what's in the depths of my heart, I ask Him to take the burden away and show me His grace instead. And with His grace, I see the goodness of a world in which cancer is taking over my mom's body.

God's grace is Him painting the sky in beautiful colors that I get to adore every evening. God's grace is Him granting the world with the hilarious actors of my favorite sitcoms. God's grace is Him instilling the confidence I need to rock red lipstick everyday. God's grace is Him placing me at a school a short hour-and-45-minutes away, so that I may spend time with my family every weekend.

God's grace is Him making my mom stronger than I could ever be, so that she can be proof that the Lord is at work in us. Despite the fact that she is the one facing this disease, she is the one who is constantly reminding me that it will be okay, that we will be okay. God is letting His plan unfold as it should, and it is unfolding perfectly, even when it doesn't feel so perfect. We learn to live with the hard when we learn to live with the grace.

"Forget the former things; do not dwell on the past. See, I am doing a new thing! Now it springs up; do you not perceive it? I am making a way in the wilderness and streams in the wasteland."
Isaiah 43:18-19

Grace is all around us all the time. It's what helps us see God at work, even in the trials in our lives. It's what reminds us to ask God for mercy in times of hard and praise God for His goodness in times of easy. It's what proves that all moments are worth celebrating, no matter how big or how small. It's what teaches us how to look on the bright side of a dreary day. It's what drives us to love hard, so hard, on those who mean the most to us. Seeing the grace of God and living in it in our toughest situations is the hardest peace we may ever face, but it is a peace that will bring us joy.

KEY VERSES:

Psalm 119:105
James 1:2-4
1 Peter 1:6-7
Colossians 1:4-6a
Isaiah 43:18-19

DISCUSSION QUESTIONS:

+ Has there ever been a time in your life when you've given up on your faith? What separated you from God?

+ Andrea explains that during her mom's cancer battle she didn't bother spending time with God and in the Word. Instead, she did everything she could to distract herself from the situation entirely. What do you use to distract yourself from pain? When life throws you difficult situations do you find yourself running towards God or away from Him?

+ The entity of all that is good, sometimes places bad in our paths: to feel an absolute need for Him, to see that His love still showers over us. When trials come, how can we posture our hearts to need God instead of holding onto bitterness and anger? How might the Lord be drawing you closer to Him in this season?

+ How is God showing you grace in unexpected places, in the mundane, and in the everyday? If you choose to see His grace in all things, how might this bring you peace in the midst of hard times?

+ Instead of dwelling on the difficulties of this world, how can you live with an eternal mindset? How might this change the way you view trails and allow you to live with more purpose?

DEVOTIONALS

DEVOTIONAL CONTRIBUTOR: *Kelsey King*

DAY 1

We humans are not much fond of pain. We would rather slide along in this life, devoid of any hurt, any harm, and anything that gives us the least bit discomfort. In an ever-buzzing world, it is becoming easier and easier to do so. Why sit in silence and take note of the loneliness that rises up inside of us when there's an ever-changing Instagram feed that fits perfectly in the palms of our hands with beautiful pictures and happy thoughts? There is always something new on our many screens at which to look, something fresh to take our mind off the inevitable hurt we feel from being a human being in a broken world.

God took on the form of a human being in Jesus, so He has a clue about what it means to hurt like we do. He knows the feeling of rejection, heartache, and that particular grief when something did not turn out how He had hoped it would. Often, feelings of being misunderstood separate us from our people in times of our deepest pain. But with God? We need not fear that misunderstanding.

Take a deep breath, embrace the quiet, and see what can be found beneath the surface. It might end up being a little scary, as hurt, loneliness and sadness tend to be, but God promises to be nearest to us when we're feeling just that. He's mighty for the burden.

KEY VERSES:
"Be still, and know that I am God."
Psalm 46:10a

"Surely he took up our pain and bore our suffering, yet we considered him punished by God, stricken by him, and afflicted. But he was pierced for our transgressions, he was crushed for our iniquities; the punishment that brought us peace was on him, and by his wounds we are healed."
Isaiah 53:4-5

REFLECTION QUESTIONS:

+ Has there ever been a time in your life when you've given up on your faith? What separated you from God?

+ Andrea explains that during her mom's cancer battle she didn't bother spending time with God and in the Word. Instead, she did everything she could to distract herself from the situation entirely. What do you use to distract yourself from pain? When life throws you difficult situations, do you find yourself running towards God or away from Him?

When life hands us lemons, the first instinct is not always to make lemonade. We wanted sweeter fruit and instead we got a lemon, a crummy deal in light of all of the sweetness that everyone else seemed to be handed. We pucker our lips at the sour taste and turn our backs on the Giver of the gift. We demand something else.

Be not mistaken—God wants to know the true feelings of our hearts. If the best we can give to Him is a puckered face and an ungrateful attitude, He will take it with the joy of a Father who gets to know His child, even on her worst days. But He has also given us an opportunity to delight in knowing that our Lord wants us to fall on Him with all we've got when we've got precisely nothing left.

Imagine the joy of a Father whose daughter knows her place in His arms when the day has gone all wrong. In trial, we're given an opportunity to both feel our feelings and also trust God with our lives, a great mystery that they do not negate one another. When trial comes, and it will, bring all of your mess and your muck to Jesus, lay it at His feet, and see with gratitude the sweetness He can make out of the most sour situation.

KEY VERSES:
"I am the good shepherd; I know my sheep and my sheep know me—just as the Father knows me and I know the Father—and I lay down my life for the sheep."
John 10:14-15

REFLECTION QUESTIONS
+ The entity of all that is good, sometimes places bad in our paths: to feel an absolute need for Him, to see that His love still showers over us. When trials come, how can we posture our hearts to need God instead of holding onto bitterness and anger? How might the Lord be drawing you closer to Him in this season?

DAY 3

When we think of grace, we do not always think of rain. But rain is grace as much as sunshine, as much as snow on a December day, as much as the sand on the beach between our toes. Somewhere, somehow, it is sustaining someone. And so it is grace, and we say amen. When we think of grace, we do not always think of rice. But rice is grace as much as the best burger in town, as much as those fancy lattes, as much as a bowl of soup thick with noodles. Somewhere, somehow, it is sustaining someone. And so it is grace, and we say amen. When we think of grace, we do not always think of pain. But pain is grace as much as joy, as much as laughter, as much as the feeling of knowing deep love. Somewhere, somehow, it is sanctifying someone. And so it is grace, and we say amen. Grace does not always look like we think it will, and we often claim it to be only the things that are the sweetest of them all. But, really, God's grace is pretty much anywhere and everywhere. His love, His grace, pulses through the earth, and it is no accident we can know Him in all things. He is not isolated to one spot, but rather, pervasive across the earth and amidst the skies, eager to shower His children. Thank God we live in a world where not only the loveliest, darling-est things get to be means of His love, but even rice and even rain and even pain too.

KEY VERSES:
"He is before all things, and in him all things hold together."
Colossians 1:17

REFLECTION QUESTIONS:
+ How is God showing you grace in unexpected places, in the mundane, and in the everyday? If you choose to see His grace in all things, how might this bring you peace in the midst of hard times?

DAY 4

One day there will not be any pain, no sorrow, and instead what will take its place is a great and wild rejoicing. We will all be with our King, and we will not have to wonder for a second if He is as good as we hoped. We will know not only in part but in full, and eternity will carry on and us with it, but we will not for a second have any notion of time. We will simply be glad to rest in the arms of our Lord.

Of course, most days right here and now, eternity is our far-off hope, out of reach just enough to cause us ache. We hear of a coming kingdom but seem to consume so little sustenance in a thirsty world. How can God expect us to trust in Him when eternity seems like, just that, an eternity away? How are we supposed to set our minds on things eternal when so much is begging for our attention right now? How are we supposed to trust him through the storm?

When your mind is heavy-laden and your heart downtrodden, remember the first things first. Faith, hope, and love are the first things, the essentials of God's character. There are so many things vying for our attention as we march on towards eternity. But the way of Christ is a simple way: have faith, bear hope, and love one another. And before too long, we'll meet Him face to face and finally understand what all the fuss was about.

KEY VERSES:
"For now we see only a reflection as in a mirror; then we shall see face to face. Now I know in part; then I shall know fully, even as I am fully known. And now these three remain: faith, hope and love. But the greatest of these is love."
1 Corinthians 13:12-13

REFLECTION QUESTIONS:
+ Instead of dwelling on the difficulties of this world, how can you live with an eternal mindset? How might this change the way you view trials and allow you to live with more purpose?

UNIVERSITY OF INDIANAPOLIS
PSYCHOLOGY
SOPHOMORE

Choosing to Rejoice

LETTING GO OF OUR CONSTANTS TO CHOOSE JOY IN CHRIST

My life has been surrounded by "constants." I constantly crave ice cream every night before bed. I constantly drop my phone or keys and break something. I constantly have moments where I look at my life and think how lucky and blessed I am. I've constantly been a part of a loving and supportive circle of people that have loved and encouraged me well. My whole life I've been drenched in constant love from family and friends, constant places where I feel welcomed, and constant reassurance from God.

So imagine my shock when my constants fell through.

My sophomore year was on the horizon, and summer was slowly fading away. I was excited about this year; I had a place of my own, and I could learn how to "adult." I was excited to see the dynamic of how living with people worked, and learning the life lessons about having roommates. I was excited for another constant. Honestly I thought that we would be attached at the hip. I thought we would make dinner together, have a tradition of watching movies every Thursday night as a reward because we had almost finished the week. Little did I know that this new constant wouldn't feel like one for much longer.

As soon as school started, things got heavy and tense between my roommates and I. I don't know exactly how it happened, but there was something that didn't feel the same. The atmosphere in our house felt heavy, and I didn't feel welcomed in my own home—I wouldn't even call it a home. I avoided going there as much as possible, and when I was there, I would lock myself in my room and wouldn't come out unless I had to go to the bathroom. I had multiple conversations with my roommates asking if there was something wrong between us, and I got nothing from these conversations. Soon after, things would just go back to the same old ways. I cried everyday. It got to the point where my anxiety was so bad that I wanted to skip class, and the classes I did go to, typically resulted in a panic attack and half the time I had to leave.

After a while I became bitter. Bitter towards the Lord, bitter towards my roommates, and bitter towards my family. Why was this happening?

When the semester ended, I was more than ready for a break. I was ready to recuperate and be surrounded by comfort and my constants again. During the break I spent a lot of time discussing and praying with my family regarding what to do about the situation... should I break the lease or push through until the end of the school year? It was hard, but at the end of the day, I had to stay in my living situation for the rest of the year. This made going back to school so much harder.

A few days before school started, I was at my friend's house with other friends and were having a conversation about how our first semester of school was a lot more difficult than we expected. They told me about how they had a conversation about wanting to start choosing joy in their day-to-day lives, rather than focusing on the negatives in life. They were not thrilled with their living situation either. I thought that their idea of choosing joy sounded impossible. Like seriously, who chooses to be happy all the time? I enjoy moping around sometimes. I enjoy not being happy all the time; it makes me feel like I am human. But I decided to join the challenge because honestly, I had nothing to lose.

My journey of choosing joy wasn't the easiest thing in the world. The first thing I realized was that there are two different types of joy: joy in the world and joy in the Lord. I realized that through my bitterness and anger from the previous semester, I was trying to put my joy in things of this world. I was putting my joy in the place that I lived and the people I lived with, and I ended up disappointed and discouraged. People *can* choose joy through the world, but the thing about choosing it through the world is that it is only temporary. Putting your joy in worldly things will let you down time-and-time again, but God's presence and grace is constant.

"Do not store up for yourselves treasures on earth, where moths and vermin destroy, and where thieves break in and steal. But store up for yourselves treasures in heaven, where moths and vermin do not destroy, and where thieves do not break in and steal. For where your treasure is, there your heart will be also."
Matthew 6:19-21

And then there is choosing joy in the Lord. The Lord does not disappoint. The Lord does not leave you, and the Lord is constant. The characteristics of the world and the Lord are complete opposites. (One constant that I know I can always count on is the Lord.)

"I will sing of the LORD's great love forever; with my mouth I will make your faithfulness known through all generations."
Psalm 89:1

When I think of the word, 'joy,' I think of two people, Apostle Paul from the Bible and my fearless father. They both have this distinct characteristic that no matter what the circumstance is, whether they hear bad news or great news, they have this inexplicable joy within them. Paul was in jail for years, and he still choose to have joy in the Lord through his hardships. Paul was in one of the scariest places you could be, but he chose to still put his trust in God and choose joy everyday.

If anyone were to meet my father, one of the first things that you would recognize is his contagious joy. When people are in the room with him, they can't help but smile. I swear his smile can be give light within a ten-mile radius of my house. He exudes contentment and energy in every word he speaks and look he gives. But the thing is, my dad was not always joyful in the Lord but rather in the world. Back in college, my dad got into some things that weren't the best. He was sad, and to fill this void, he turned to drugs and drinking alcohol, which he thought would give him joy. Unfortunately, none of these things filled that sadness but made him more angry and bitter. He was so fed-up with this feeling of hopelessness and depression that he decided it would be best to end his life. The day he planned to do this though, God had a great and different plan. I won't play out the rest of the story, but the Lord was there that day.

"Fill my heart with joy when their grain and new wine abound. In peace I will lie down and sleep, for you alone, LORD, make me dwell in safety."
Psalm 4:7-8

My dad later realized that all of these things he was putting his joy in were not satisfying his needs. It was a process, but over time, he ended up satisfied in the Lord "for He is good," as he would say. Today my dad chooses joy every single day.

Although my story about finding joy is different than my dad's, the one part of our journey in common that led us on the path of joy was finding ourselves. I thought my living situation my sophomore year was going to be one more blessing that I could add to my ever-growing list of constants in my life. When that turned out to be the opposite of true and so much of my comfort zone had been stripped away from me, I felt for the first time in my life desperate for God. I was desperate for His comfort and His constant source of love, grace, and truth in my life. I knew that only God could fill the void in my heart that my tough situation with my roommates had created. I knew that only through God could I find joy in that situation.

I encourage you to pray for that desperation, and let the Lord break you, so that you can turn to Him and choose the Joy through Him. I encourage you to put reminders up in places you will see multiple times a day about choosing joy, whether that be sticky notes, the background of your phone, or even a cute bracelet. Whatever works for you—do it because I promise it will make an impact on your attitude towards choosing joy. Joy is such a small word but has such a huge meaning when you find it in the Lord.

"For in the day of trouble he will keep me safe in his dwelling; he will hide me in the shelter of his sacred tent and set me high upon a rock. Then my head will be exalted above the enemies who surround me; at his sacred tent I will sacrifice with shouts of joy; I will sing and make music to the Lord. Hear my voice when I call, Lord; be merciful to me and answer me."
Psalm 27:5-7

I wish I could say that choosing joy everyday has been a piece of cake, but that would be the furthest thing from the truth. There are days where I still feel like an alien in my own home, and I'm frustrated with my roommates and the feeling I get when I walk in my front door. Those are the days that the absolute last thing I want to do is choose joy. But I find that when I do, God typically shows up in the most unexpected ways. On some of my worst days, I've ended up having incredible conversations with one of my roommates. I've been given opportunities to serve my roommates or to be there for them when normally I would just set myself in my room. God has begun to mend and heal brokenness in my home.

I think when we choose joy in all things God doesn't necessarily change our situations, but He changes our outlook. That is enough to change everything.

The Lord broke me. He took me in and comforted me. The Lord gives me the choice to choose joy everyday. Today I wake up and choose joy. I hear some not so great news, and I try to always find joy in that situation. It's not easy, but it never fails to prove to be worth it, for my God is good.

"Rejoice always…"
1 Thessalonians 5:16

What a simple verse, but what an amazing message! Rejoice when you're in a sticky situation. Rejoice when you've had a rough day. Even rejoice when you slept through your alarm. Whatever the circumstance, rejoice for God calls us to do so.

"Clap your hands, all you nations; shout to God with cries of joy."
Psalm 47:1

KEY VERSES:
Matthew 6:19-21
Psalm 89:1
Psalm 4:7-8
Psalm 27:5-7
1 Thessalonians 5:16
Psalm 47:1

DISCUSSION QUESTIONS:

+ What are the constants in your life—the things that keep you comfortable and secure? When things get tough, what do you find yourself leaning on?

+ Erin shares about how her difficult roommate situation placed her outside of her comfort zone and desperate for God. Has your comfort zone kept you from needing the Lord? How can stepping away from your constants deepen intimacy with God?

+ What things, other than Christ, do you believe will bring you joy? How often do you turn to these things instead of Christ? When you turn to these things, how does it leave you feeling?

+ Is there somebody in your life who exudes joy in all things? How does their joy affect you and the people around them?

+ When you choose joy in all things, God doesn't always change your situations, but He changes your outlook. Regardless of the circumstance, how can you rejoice in the Lord today? What things can you do to remind yourself and others to always choose joy in Christ?

DEVOTIONALS

DEVOTIONAL CONTRIBUTOR: *Sarah Buchanan*

DAY 1

College is such an unknown, so naturally we craft our dream scenarios of what classes will be like, what color scheme our dorm will have, and if our roommate will be our new best friend. We think about how we will fill our schedules with yoga classes and coffee shop dates. By the end of the whole experience, we will understand what those grown-ups said about this being "the best years of our lives."

In Erin's story, we read of her excitement for the school year ahead and her goals of learning how to "adult" and live with roommates. She was ready to put that check mark in the box and add this as another "constant" in her life, alongside craving ice cream and feeling the love of God. To her dismay, reality stepped in and threw her "constants" aside.

It is so easy to lean on what we know and are familiar with. Yet, these very things can be getting in the way of trusting in the God who understands our situation far better than we ever could. Our "constants" that feel so safe can come crashing down in an instant and leave us outside of our comfort zone. In that moment, we have two choices—to sulk and become bitter at our situation or choose to dig in deeper to His Word and try to focus on what He is teaching us. Your situations will never be constant, but your God always will.

KEY VERSES:
"Trust in the LORD with all your heart and lean not on your own understanding; in all your ways submit to him, and he will make your paths straight."
Proverbs 3:5-6

"Make every effort to live in peace with everyone and to be holy; without holiness no one will see the Lord. See to it that no one falls short of the grace of God and that no bitter root grows up to cause trouble and defile many."
Hebrews 12:14-15

REFLECTION QUESTIONS:

+ What are the constants in your life—the things that keep you comfortable and secure? When things get tough, what do you find yourself leaning on?

+ Erin shares about how her difficult roommate situation placed her outside of her comfort zone and desperate for God. Has your comfort zone kept you from needing the Lord? How can stepping away from your constants deepen intimacy with God?

DAY 2

In Erin's story, she mentions two types of joy: joy in the world and joy in the Lord. Take a moment to pause and jot down what you believe are some differences between those two. Joy in the world and what it has to offer is not inherently bad, but it can distract us from the Giver of those joys. Not to mention, worldly joys are temporary and cannot sustain us.

Do you ebb and flow according to your living arrangements, how your friends are treating you, or even if you got that A on your paper? When we are searching for joy in what the world can offer us, we will always come up short. Today, let us fix our eyes on what is eternal. Let us choose to rejoice in God because joy in Him is one constant you can add to your list forever.

KEY VERSES:
"So we fix our eyes not on what is seen, but on what is unseen, since what is seen is temporary, but what is unseen is eternal."
2 Corinthians 4:18

"Do not store up for yourselves treasures on earth, where moths and vermin destroy, and where thieves break in and steal. But store up for yourselves treasures in heaven, where moths and vermin do not destroy, and where thieves do not break in and steal. For where your treasure is, there your heart will be also."
Matthew 6:19-21

REFLECTION QUESTIONS:
+ What things, other than Christ, do you believe will bring you joy? How often do you turn to these things instead of Christ? When you turn to these things, how does it leave you feeling?

There are so many ways to define joy: It's easy to spot in a smile or a laugh, but it's also found in those moments where you feel God whispering "I love you" as you look out to the most beautiful sunrise or when you find ten extra minutes in your jam-packed day. Joy is a posture of the heart, and it is something that we as Christians should be striving towards every day.

Yesterday you reflected on some things you believe will bring you joy; so today dive deeper into what genuine joy looks like.

One of the people Erin mentions as having contagious joy is the Apostle Paul. In the Bible when we read of the crazy life of Paul, it feels like the bigger the trial he faces, the more joy he is able to exude. How does that math add up? Paul knew the secret to genuine and contagious joy. He knew that trials were going to come, and he was prepared to face them. He had joy in spite of trouble because he knew that God's purpose was still progressing. We, too, have a reason to rejoice always if we believe that no matter the circumstance, God is still at work within us and within the world.

KEY VERSES:
"Rejoice always, pray continually, and give thanks in all circumstances; for this is God's will for you in Christ Jesus."
1 Thessalonians 5:16-18

"Therefore we do not lose heart. Though outwardly we are wasting away, yet inwardly we are being renewed day by day. For our light and momentary troubles are achieving for us an eternal glory that far outweighs them all."
2 Corinthians 4:16-17

REFLECTION QUESTIONS:
+ Is there somebody in your life who exudes joy in all things? How does their joy affect you and the people around them?
surrender to God today?

DAY 4

It is really easy to go through our days without noticing the beauty and joy right in front of us. We are often so busy trying to stay focused on our schedule and our endless 'to-do' list that we lose focus of the abundant blessings God is pouring out over our lives. We have been taking a deeper look at joy this week and what it means in our own lives. The final question we are left with is how can we live this out in every season. We know how to rejoice when life seems to be going our way because it is a natural response. The tricky part comes when our world shatters into a tiny million pieces, and we have no idea how we could possibly muster up a sliver of joy.

Re-read Erin's story today and focus on her plea—that you would pray to God for desperation and longing to crave more of Him. When we seek our Father's heart in the hard times, we are seeking refuge and shelter from the storm. It is in these moments that He can carry our hearts and find our song of joy that was hidden in the darkest part of us. Take some time over the next few days to jot down the times you chose to be bitter over rejoicing. Then, begin asking our Father what it looks like to choose joy every single time. Get honest with yourself and with Him and watch the fruit of your labor come to pass.

May we look to defeats and trials as an opportunity, not a road block. May we choose joy when it doesn't seem possible. This life is not guaranteed to be trouble-free, but joy is promised to come in the morning.

KEY VERSES:
"There is a time for everything, and a season for every activity under the heavens…a time to weep and a time to laugh, a time to mourn and a time to dance…"
Ecclesiastes 3:1, 4

"Sing the praises of the Lord, you his faithful people; praise his holy name. For his anger lasts only a moment, but his favor lasts a lifetime; weeping may stay for the night, but rejoicing comes in the morning."
Psalm 30:4-5

REFLECTION QUESTIONS:
+ When you choose joy in all things, God doesn't always change your situations, but He changes your outlook. Regardless of the circumstance, how can you rejoice in the Lord today? What things can you do to remind yourself and others to always choose joy in Christ?

YOU ARE ONE IN A MELON

FROM: Love
      Your Melon